HISTORIES OF THE UNEXPECTED

The Tudors

By the same authors

Histories of the Unexpected

In the same series

Histories of the Unexpected: The Vikings
Histories of the Unexpected: World War II
Histories of the Unexpected: The Romans

HISTORIES OF THE UNEXPECTED

The Tudors

Sam Willis & James Daybell

Atlantic Books
London

First published in Great Britain in 2019 by Atlantic Books,
an imprint of Atlantic Books Ltd.

1 2 3 4 5 6 7 8 9

A CIP catalogue record for this book is available from
the British Library.

Hardback ISBN: 978-1-78649-769-7
E-book ISBN: 978-1-78649-770-3

Printed and bound by CPI Group (UK) Ltd, Croydon, CR0 4YY

Atlantic Books
An Imprint of Atlantic Books Ltd
Ormond House
26–27 Boswell Street
London
WC1N 3JZ

www.atlantic-books.co.uk

For

Kate	*Felix*
&	*&*
Alice	*Bea*

CONTENTS

Everything

HAS A

history

EVEN THE MOST

unexpected

OF SUBJECTS...

... and *everything*

LINKS TOGETHER

IN

unexpected

WAYS

A PERSONAL NOTE

At *Histories of the Unexpected*, we believe that *everything* has a history – even the most unexpected of subjects – and that everything links together in unexpected ways.

We believe that the itch, crawling, clouds, lightning, zombies and zebras and holes and perfume and rubbish and mustard – each has a fascinating history of its own.

In this book we take this approach into the Tudor world. You will find out how the history of *shrinking* is all to do with the Spanish Armada; how the history of *oranges* is all about Tudor spies; and how the history of *monsters* is connected to those famous Tudor queens Mary I and Elizabeth I.

To explore and enjoy subjects in this way will change not only how you think about the past, but also the present. It is enormously rewarding, and we encourage you all to join in! Find us online at www.historiesoftheunexpected.com and on Twitter @UnexpectedPod – and do please get in touch.

ACKNOWLEDGEMENTS

This series of books is about sharing great research and new approaches to history. Our first acknowledgement, therefore, must go to all of those brilliant historians – professional and amateur – who are writing today and who are changing the way that we think about the past. You are all doing a fabulous job, and one which often goes unremarked and unrewarded. Thank you for your time, effort, energy and insight. We could not have written this book without you.

Since this book is intended for a wide and general audience, we have chosen not to publish with extensive footnotes. We acknowledge our indebtedness to fellow historians in the Selected Further Reading section at the end of the book, which is also intended as a spur to further research for our readers.

We would like to thank the many colleagues and friends who have generously offered ideas, guidance, support and sustenance – intellectual and otherwise: Andy Gordon, Nadine Akkerman, Sue Broomhall, Anthony Caleshu, Erika Gaffney, Lee Jane Giles, Emma Haddon, Dan Maudlin, Angela McShane, Elaine Murphy, Svante Norrhem, the Lord John Russell, Adam Smyth, Jacqueline Van Gent, Suzie Lipscomb, Janina Ramirez, Phillip Northcott, Darius Arya, James Holland, Michael Duffy, Andrew Lambert and Jennie Stogdon; and among the twitterati, @HunterSJones, @RedLunaPixie, @KittNoir and @Kazza2014.

Collective thanks are also due to Dan Snow, Tom Clifford and the fabulous History Hit team for all their support and encouragement, as well as to Will Atkinson, James Nightingale, Kate Straker, Jamie Forrest, Gemma Wain and everyone at Atlantic Books.

We would also like to thank everyone (and there are hundreds of thousands of you) who has listened to the podcast or come to see one of our live events and been so charming and enthusiastic.

Most of all, however, we would like to thank our families, young and old, for everything they have done and continue to do, to cope with – of *all things* – a historian in their lives ...

But we have created this book for you.

Sam and James

Isca – Escanceaster – Exeter
The Feast of St Benedict – 8-Dhū al-Qa'dah 1440 – I.VII.MMXIX – 11 July 2019

THE TUDORS: AN INTRODUCTION

The family of Henry VIII: *An Allegory of the Tudor Succession* by Lucas de Heere

WHO WERE THEY?

The Tudor dynasty ruled England from 1485 to 1603. It was preceded by the House of York – whose reign ended with Richard III's defeat at the Battle of Bosworth, finally bringing the lengthy Wars of the Roses (1455–87) to a close – and was succeeded by James VI and I, and the House of Stuart.

Henry VII (1485–1509)

Henry VIII (1509–47)

Edward VI (1547–53) | **Mary I (1553–58)** | **Elizabeth I (1558–1603)**

MONARCHY

Henry VII

Tudor rule began with a military victory at the Battle of Bosworth in 1485, when the forces of the Welsh-born Henry Tudor, a man with a weak hereditary claim to the throne, won against all odds. Richard III was slain on the battlefield, and the 'Welsh usurper' became Henry VII, establishing a dynasty that ruled for almost 120 years.

Henry ruled from 1485 to 1509. He set about consolidating power at home and abroad, putting down rebellions and fending off pretenders to the throne. A bureaucratic king, when he died he bequeathed a country that was solvent and secure – and, importantly, had Tudor heirs to succeed him on the throne.

Henry VIII

Henry was succeeded by his son Henry VIII (1509–47), an egotistical maniac famed for his six wives: Catherine of Aragon (divorced), Anne Boleyn (beheaded), Jane Seymour (died), Anne of Cleves (divorced), Catherine Howard (beheaded) and Katherine Parr (survived). He is also famed for his split from the Roman Catholic Church in 1533, after which he established the Church of England, setting himself up as its supreme head, and dissolved the monasteries.

Henry took great interest in three things – his love life, religion and war – but he is a remarkably difficult king to fathom: a man of tempestuous emotions and feelings, who drew people very close only to later destroy them.

Edward VI

Henry VIII was succeeded by his three children. Edward VI (1547–53), born to Jane Seymour and educated as a Protestant, ascended the throne at the age of nine and died of tuberculosis six years later. His rule was dominated by regency government, first led by his uncle Edward Seymour, Duke of Somerset and Lord Protector of England, then by John Dudley, Duke of Northumberland.

These two imposing figures governed during Edward's minority, although evidence of the king's journal shows a developing political experience and precocious personality. Both Somerset and Northumberland were executed for trying to seize power, the latter attempting to place Lady Jane Grey on the throne, having married her to his son, Lord Guildford Dudley. The unfortunate Jane, who was little more than a political pawn, ruled for just nine days before being executed.

Mary I

Mary I (1553–58), daughter of Henry's first wife, Catherine of Aragon, was the first woman to rule the country, if we discount the disputed and short-lived reigns of Empress Matilda in 1141 and Lady Jane Grey in 1553. Her gender, Spanish husband and Catholic faith drew criticism from those who wished to see a return to Protestant rule.

She has been unfairly tarred with the epithet 'Bloody Mary' for her persecution of Protestant heretics. Her reign was dominated by religion, her marriage to Philip II of Spain, and an unsuccessful war against France which resulted in the loss of Calais. In 1554 she put down an armed rebellion led by Sir Thomas Wyatt.

Mary died in pain during the 1558 flu epidemic that took so many lives, after just five years of rule. With no heir, the throne fell to her Protestant half-sister, Elizabeth.

Elizabeth I

Elizabeth, daughter of the beheaded Anne Boleyn, is one of the longest-ruling monarchs in Britain's history. Her reign, which is often viewed as a 'golden age', lasted from 1558 to 1603.

Unlike her warmonger father, Elizabeth is famous for trying to stay out of expensive armed conflicts. She nearly died of smallpox in 1562, and the first half of her rule was marked by a series of high-profile courtships. She signed the death warrant for the execution of her fellow monarch Mary, Queen of Scots, and repelled the Spanish Armada in 1588.

She remained unmarried and childless. Upon her death, the Tudor dynasty ended and the crown passed to the House of Stuart in the hands of her cousin James VI of Scotland, whose claim to the English throne was through his great-grandmother Margaret Tudor, sister of Henry VIII.

POLITICAL POWER

In the world of Tudor politics, the monarch was all-powerful, the linchpin of the entire system. Each monarch brought in their own particular flavour of governance, influenced by their character, age and gender.

Parliament was weak, and power was concentrated in the hands of a small number of government ministers and courtiers – who advised the monarch, and devised and implemented policy. Many of the monarchs' reigns were characterized by warring factions of these ministers and courtiers, which made politics violent and bloody.

RELIGION

The Tudor world contained a bizarre mixture of religion and superstition. Throughout the sixteenth century, traditional spiritual teachings coexisted alongside alternative beliefs: witchcraft and magic, old wives' tales, superstition and the paranormal.

The Tudor period was dominated by the Reformation, which created a schism within the Christian Church between Catholics and those who wanted reform. Those living throughout these years experienced a rollercoaster in terms of faith, as the changing loyalties of the various Tudor monarchs veered the country between Catholicism and Protestantism.

In 1533, Henry VIII divorced his first wife, Catherine of Aragon, and split from the Church of Rome. He established the Church of England, dissolved the monasteries – plundering their wealth – and executed high-profile opponents who refused to accept him as the head of the Church.

Under Edward VI, religion took a sharper swing towards Protestantism. Educated by Protestant tutors, it was intended that Edward's rule would secure a true religious reformation. Two new Books of Common Prayer were introduced, and a series of reforms stripped away the trappings of Catholic worship. Churches were whitewashed, images and 'superstitious' rituals were destroyed. Edward's untimely death, however, brought an end to the Protestant evangelism of his reign.

Mary I restored traditional Catholic worship, renewing the relationship with the Church of Rome, and she even attempted to re-endow monastic lands. Over the course of her reign, more than 800 Protestants fled into exile and some 300 were executed as heretics. During this time, however, the Church was beset by financial and administrative weaknesses, and ultimately by Mary's untimely death.

The situation changed yet again under the Protestant Elizabeth I, who did more than anyone else to establish the Anglican Church. But not everyone found what they wanted in this newly defined Church of England, and there was significant domestic turmoil among Protestants – as well as between Protestants and Catholics. It also made her enemies abroad. The pope excommunicated Elizabeth in 1570, which led to a wave of attempts on the monarch's life and threats of invasion – the most famous of which was in 1588 when the Spanish Armada set sail, intent on landing an army on English soil.

CULTURE

The Tudor period was culturally rich and vibrant. The creative arts thrived and produced some of the greatest poets and writers the English language has ever seen, such as William Shakespeare, Edmund Spenser and John Donne. It also saw increasing levels of education and literacy in all ranks of society. Print flourished and books circulated in ever greater numbers, spreading knowledge, ideas and news.

SOCIETY

There were strict divisions between the ruling and subordinate classes in Tudor society. At the apex was the royal family, followed by the nobility and gentry, then yeomen and citizens, then labourers, and at the bottom of the heap, paupers and vagrants. Deeply patriarchal, women and children were viewed as significantly inferior to men within the family and in society at large.

Married women could not own property in their own right, and girls were excluded from most formal educational institutions. Conduct manuals widely held that women should be chaste, silent and obedient, but in practice women were able to negotiate power at a local level, especially within marriage and the family.

Both the Church and the state regulated behaviour at all levels of society and across a wide range of areas, from witchcraft and heresy, defamation and slander, to sex, work and even rowdy drinking on a Sunday. Execution, imprisonment and financial penalties sat alongside other forms of social control that sought to ritually humiliate the accused.

EXPLORATION

This was a time of great discovery. Equipped with better ships than ever before, explorers discovered unknown parts of the world – and Francis Drake even sailed around it. This burgeoning knowledge of the wider world led to a new interest in expanding English control overseas, a subsequent growth in empire, and new reasons for conflict both at home and abroad.

AN UNEXPECTED APPROACH

Traditionally, the Tudors have been understood in a very straightforward way, following the well-known personalities, events and themes. We think, however, that the period really comes alive if you take an *unexpected* approach to its history.

Yes, Tudor monarchs, exploration and religion have a fascinating history, but so too do cannibalism, shrinking, bells, hats, mirrors, monsters, oranges, doors, faces, accidents, toilets, fire, lists, gifts, windows, chairs, bones, eyes, letter-writing and even fruit-eating!

Each of these subjects is fascinating in its own right, and each also sheds new light on the traditional subjects and themes that we think we know so well.

Are you sitting comfortably? Then let's start with the history of the chair...

·1·

THE CHAIR

A woodcut of a cucking stool originally printed in *A Strange and Wonderful Relation of the Old Woman Who Was Drowned at Ratcliff-Highway* (London, no date)

In the Tudor world, chairs were used to control the public…

DUCKING AND CUCKING

In the Tudor world, chairs were used to control the public, and the ducking stool was the most extreme example. Used to punish a variety of offences – including scolding, illegitimacy, prostitution and witchcraft – the ducking stool was built like a wooden see-saw, with a chair at one end of the 'lever'. The accused would be tied to this chair and plunged into water, usually by raising up the lever's opposite end. According to Tudor legal commentators, the suspect was 'to be ducked over the head and ears into the water'. The nature of this act of immersion depended on the nature of the crime – it could be a short sharp shock for minor offences, or continually repeated throughout the day in more severe cases. On occasion, the punishment was fatal.

Closely related was the cucking stool, which, far more simply, was used for ritual humiliation: the individual was forced to sit in the chair in a public place as an act of penance, in full view of passers-by. Designed to shame, it worked in much the same way as other forms of rough justice.

In the Tudor period, ducking and cucking stools were used to punish troublesome and angry women – commonly termed 'scolds' – who had caused social disorder. While they were also the fate of brawling men, and male traders who cheated the public by selling short measures or adulterated food, over the course of the sixteenth century such stools became increasingly associated with the abuse of women. As with the scold's bridle, metal headgear which included a plate that fitted in the mouth to restrain a prattling tongue, they were used to control what was deemed wayward female behaviour.

Rough justice

Rough justice in the Tudor world was the heavy-handed, harsh punishments that were meted out instead of fining or imprisonment. Many offenders were wheeled around in an open wooden cart; others were placed in a pillory, a large hinged wooden board with holes for securing the head and hands, or stocks, which restrained the feet. These were erected in public spaces, and passers-by could insult, spit at, taunt or even hurl fruit at the imprisoned occupants.

WITCHES

Ducking stools were also used as a test for women accused of witchcraft: those who rose to the surface when immersed were deemed to be guilty, the Devil conspiring in saving them; while those who sank were drowned but with their innocence intact.

Another coercive type of chair was the 'interrogation stool', on which those accused of witchcraft were forced to sit as they were questioned about their supposed crimes. We know of the existence of such stools from Shakespeare's *Troilus and Cressida* (Act II, Scene i), when Ajax issues the insult 'Thou stool for a witch!'

An example of a witch's interrogation stool survives in the

cottage of Shakespeare's wife, Anne Hathaway, in the Warwickshire village of Shottery. Carved from oak and ash and with four legs, the most fascinating aspect of the stool is the five sets of concentric circles carved into the seat. They resemble the ring patterns commonly found on wooden mantelpieces, beams and door lintels of Tudor properties; known as 'witch-marks', these were believed to ward off evil spirits.

Witch-mark found on beam in a sixteenth-century house in Herefordshire, UK

The presence of such markings on an interrogation stool was supposed to neutralize the occult power of the witch when she was forced to sit, often tied to the stool, for interminable periods of time. While it is difficult to reconstruct what that experience was like for women accused of witchcraft, the interrogation stool as an object does conjure up something of the atmosphere of the courtroom, in which the accused could be confronted by hostile audiences and were stripped and searched for another kind of witch's marks (also known as 'devil's marks'), such as an odd-looking birthmark or an extra nipple. In 1579, a court in Southampton ordered a dozen 'honest matrons' to strip-search one widow Walker and check for 'eny bludie marke on hir bodie which is a common token to know all witches by'.

THRONES

At the Tudor court, another chair, the royal throne, was used for social control in a different way. Ornately and richly decorated and raised on a plinth, the throne emanated power and grandeur. It singled out the monarch above all others, and it was also used to regulate access to them.

Several of Henry VIII's thrones survive at Hampton Court and Dover Castle, and they appear rather less grand than one might expect. Both are relatively small carved wooden chairs, upholstered in red velvet and decorated with gold braiding. There is a sense that these particular examples were functional rather than fancy – they were everyday thrones for the king.

On an entirely different level, however, were Tudor coronation thrones. A set of detailed instructions for the preparations of Westminster Cathedral for the coronation of Mary I in 1553 gives a wonderful sense of the rich opulence of the royal throne that was at the centre of a very public ceremony.

The notes describe a scaffold with a throne set at the top of seven stairs. The throne itself was 'in the midst' of it, 'a great white chair' with two pillars topped with two gold lions and a gold fleur-de-lys. It was covered with a canopy of gold cloth and furnished with two cushions, one black velvet embroidered with gold, the other of tissue. Edward VI's own coronation throne included the addition of two cushions 'to help raise the small King'.

THE PRESENCE CHAMBER

The significant role of the throne continued long after the coronation ceremony. For Tudor courtiers, the ability to move from public areas to the more private spaces connected with the monarch was a sign of royal favour. Central to this procession of power was the presence chamber – the room where the monarch received visitors – and the key piece of furniture here was the throne and canopy (or 'chair and cloth' of state), upon which the monarch sat.

To be rescinded access to the monarch's presence on his or her throne was to fall from political favour. And that fall could be hard. Robert Devereux, 2nd Earl of Essex – who was executed for treason in 1601 – was denied admission to Queen Elizabeth late in 1599 after he deserted his military command in Ireland. For Essex, the fact that he would no longer see the queen on her throne was a sign of ill things to come.

Robert Devereux (1565–1601)

The Earl of Essex was an English nobleman, military commander and royal favourite of Elizabeth I. He was put under house arrest in 1599 as a result of his poor military leadership in Ireland during the Nine Years' War. Frozen out of the queen's favour, Essex attempted to march on the court in order to try to capture the queen and seize power for himself and his supporters. The coup failed, and Essex was arrested, put on trial and beheaded.

Exactly who was allowed to approach the throne in the Tudor period was thus strictly controlled, so much so that in Elizabeth I's reign one of her Gentleman Ushers of the Chamber, Simon Bowyer, was ordered by the queen to deny access to anyone without proper papers. He incurred the wrath of the Earl of Leicester on one occasion when he refused access to one of the earl's known clients, yet the queen herself backed up Bowyer, emphasizing that she alone decided who had the privilege of time with her as monarch, seated on her throne.

·2·

MONSTERS

Woodcut of Argus sea monster in *Monstrum in Oceano Germanica* ('Monsters of the North Sea'), from Olaus Magnus, 1537

The Tudors saw monsters as a message…

PHYSICAL DEFORMITY

The Tudors viewed monsters as messages or signs that explained the world around them, and they saw them in places we do not. One of those places was in humans and animals suffering from physical defects.

Such occurrences were widely known, and were reported in printed newsbooks and pamphlets of the period. Between 1552 and 1570, sixteen 'monstrous' births were recorded and no fewer than nineteen monstrous fish were put on display.

A particularly notable year for monstrous events was 1562, as recorded by the renowned English historian and antiquarian John Stow in his *Annales of England* (1592):

> In March a Mare brought forth a foale with one body, and two heads, and as it were a long taile growing out betweene the two heads. Also a sow farrowed a pigge with foure legges like to the armes of a man child, with hands and fingers...
>
> The foure and twentieth day of May, a man childe was borne at Chichester in Sussex, the head, armes, and legges whereof, were like an Anatomie, the breast and belly monstrous big from the navell, as it were a long string hanging: about the necke a great collar of flesh & skin growing like to the ruffe of a shirt or neckerchefe, comming uppe above the eares pleyting and folding.

Such monsters represented a disruption to the 'great chain of being' that delineated the social and celestial hierarchy in the Tudor world and cosmos. In this system, everything was supposed to be neatly ordered and in its proper place – from God and the angels in heaven to the monarch and patriarchs on earth. The 'monsters' so widely reported and sensationalized represented a break in that natural order and were believed to be portents from God – signs of his displeasure.

John Stow (1525–1605)

Stow was one of England's earliest historians, and probably the most prolific historical writer of the sixteenth century. Most well-known for his *Survey of London* (1598), his books and chronicles are some of the most valuable sources in the study of Tudor England.

SIN AND JUDGEMENT

In Tudor thought, there was a strong link between sin and monstrosity – deformity being considered one of the ways in which God demonstrated his divine power to men. One pamphlet from 1569 remarks on the phenomenon of monstrous births 'so abhominable and deformed, that they seeme to be brought into the world... in contempt of nature'. These monsters thus generated a unique type of fear, for the more numerous the examples and the more extreme the deformities, the closer everyone on earth was to God's judgement and wrath.

Among medical writers, however, deformed births were considered the result of mothers who were diseased or suffered from mental illness or who engaged in sinful sexual activity, which included sex during pregnancy or menstruation (known as 'bestial intercourse'). A translation of a sixteenth-century text on the art of begetting beautiful children warned men against coitus during the menses, demonstrating how Tudor men were weighed down by patriarchal fears and disgust of menstruating women:

Press not your Wives, tho height'nd Lust incite
The Soul to try the pleasurable Fight,
While the Blood monthly rushing from the Veins,
The Flowing Womb with foul Pollution stains...
But if by Chance the Seeds concurring fix,
And with th'impurer Dross of Nature mix,
What a detested, miscreated Thing
From such ill-suited Principles must spring?

HIDDEN MONSTERS

Monsters were not simply identified by their physical deformities during the Tudor period; the imagery of monstrosity was increasingly employed to describe those whose thoughts and behaviours were diametrically opposed to one's own.

In the middle of the sixteenth century a particularly troubling type of monster appeared, as the Tudors increasingly saw monsters in people and objects that had no outwardly visible sign of deformity – a new way of seeing the world that was beautifully encapsulated in this verse from 1562, by the author William Fulwood:

And loke what great deformitie,
In bodies ye beholde:
Much more is in our mindes truly,
An hundreth thousand folde.

These were people whose moral, religious or political codes were considered suspicious or unacceptable. These were people whose beliefs or behaviour – rather than their appearance – revealed their supposedly monstrous nature; and this became a powerful tool for social commentators wanting to expose anything from heresy and treason to greed and pride. The civil lawyer Walter Haddon (1516–72), for example – in his tract *A Dialogue Agaynst the Tyrannye of the Papistes* (1562) – wrote of the 'monstrous maxims of the Popes bond men' as a way of describing what he saw as the heretical shortcomings of the Catholic faith.

The first decade or so of Elizabeth I's reign was a time of high anxiety, and historians believe that to have been reflected in this new perception of monsters. And as Elizabeth's reign progressed, there was little to lessen the unease: uncertainty increased over the absence of an heir, hunger and disease were a constant threat, England faced external aggression from Spain and the economy was weak. There was still great disquiet in certain circles, too, over Mary's restoration of Catholicism (1553–8). Such periods of political and religious turmoil encouraged conflict and disunity. In other words, this was a fertile breeding ground for monsters.

FEMALE MONARCHS

Nowhere was the growing anxiety about the dangers of monsters more acutely expressed than in the radical Scottish Reformer John Knox's polemical resistance tract *First Blast of the Trumpet Against the Monstrous Regiment of Women* (1558), in which he describes female rule as 'monstrous'.

John Knox (1513–72)

A Scottish religious Reformer who was royal chaplain under Edward VI, he spent Mary I's reign living in exile in Geneva and then Frankfurt. During this period he wrote most of his polemical works, including his best-known pamphlet, *The First Blast*. On his return to Scotland in 1559, he strongly opposed the Catholic Mary, Queen of Scots, and played an important role in the Scottish Reformation.

Knox's argument against women monarchs was based on several premises: that it was against the will of God, against the natural order of the world and against the nature of women, whom it was deemed should be chaste, silent and obedient. Drawing a parallel between the human body and the body politic, Knox considered that a country with a woman as its head of state was one that was corrupted and cankered. In the 'natural body of man', all parts were in their correct places: the head on the body, the arms and legs all where they should be, and the senses functioning normally, 'the eye [able] to see, the ear to hear, and the tongue to speak'. Likewise, a properly functioning body politic had a man as its head. With a queen on the throne, this order was distorted.

'For who would not judge', Knox wrote, 'that body to be a monster, where there was no head eminent above the rest, but that the eyes were in the hands, the tongue and the mouth beneath in the belly, and the ears in the feet? ... And no less monstrous is the body of that commonwealth where a woman bears empire.' According to him, it was nothing less than the world turned upside down.

But the Presbyterian Knox was a firebrand who had little or no support for such extreme views, and his timing was terrible. No sooner had the tract been published than the Protestant princess Elizabeth ascended the throne of England and the Church veered down a course of Anglicanism. Nonetheless, it is a powerful example of how ordinary people explained what was wrong with the world around them... with monsters.

·3·

THE TOILET

A close stool, Hampton Court Palace

The Tudor toilet was all about political power...

THE KING'S TOILET

The history of the toilet in the Tudor world is all about power and personality in Henrician England. Henry VIII is in fact jokingly referred to by some modern-day historians as the 'toilet-paper' king, and political influence was, in a manner of speaking, from the bottom upwards. Key to this intimate world of early Tudor power politics are an object and a person: the 'close stool' and the man who looked after it.

The close stool was an early portable toilet, made of wood and in the shape of a cabinet, with a lid that opened and a seat. They could be highly decorative items, as we know from a set of bills dating from 1546 that detail the making of 'a close stool for the use of the King's Majesty'. This stool was covered in black velvet and required three pounds of down for stuffing the seat, elbows and side pieces, as well as 2,000 gilt 'garnishing nails', twenty-six gold nails, and decorative silk and ribbon.

A lavish example that tells us more about such objects actually survives in the collections of Hampton Court Palace. It is a small wooden box of about seat height, upholstered in red velvet for comfort and also to disguise its purpose. It even has a lock, so its contents could remain private.

Hampton Court Palace

A magnificent royal residence on the River Thames, eleven miles south-west of central London. Built for Cardinal Wolsey in 1515, Henry VIII confiscated and later enlarged it when his chief minister fell from power.

The box would have been kept in a private room reserved solely for use by the royal behind. This room would have been furnished with washing facilities – since water and rags were used to clean Tudor backsides, in a time before disposable toilet paper – and dressed with curtains and hangings for privacy and warmth.

GROOM OF THE STOOL

Power lay not in the object itself, but in the man who accompanied the monarch when he was using the close stool. This ceremonial figure was known as the 'Groom of the Stool' – a position of immense influence within the political system, since he alone had right of entry to the king's 'bed-chamber and other privy places'.

As a close body servant of the king, the Groom of the Stool was of high social standing and privy to the most intimate functions of the royal body. In 1539 Sir Thomas Heneage, who held this position for ten years, recorded the impact of Henry VIII dosing himself with laxatives and an enema. He wrote in a letter to Henry's chief minister Thomas Cromwell that 'his Grace rose to go to the stool which, by working of the pills and glister [an enema] that his Highness had taken before, had a very fair siege'.

The Groom of the Stool also liaised with royal physicians, who measured the monarch's urine and examined his stools as an index of his overall health. This kind of detailed knowledge of the king's bowel movements had significant political importance, since the health of the monarch was seen as an indicator of the health of the nation itself.

Regular intimate access to Henry also meant that Grooms were close confidants and became figures of great influence. Henrician politics was all about personalities, and Henry was particularly swayed by those in such personal proximity to him. Sir William Compton, the first Groom of the Stool (1509–26), used the position to accumulate vast personal wealth, acquiring numerous offices and estates throughout the Midland counties by dint of his connection with the king. Regular attendance on the monarch over a lengthy period of time meant that he was able to gauge the king's mood and thus acquire the royal signature on documents giving him ownership of land. Politics as described here was less about influence over policy than about lining one's own pockets.

MINIONS

Other Grooms of the Stool used their position to acquire political power. Sir Henry Norris, who was Groom from 1526 to 1536, was among Henry VIII's closest confidants and had been one of a small handful of young courtiers – known at the time as the 'minions' – who surrounded the young Henry when he first ascended the throne in 1509. In his role, Norris was well placed to thwart or support suits to the king for royal patronage, and he controlled Privy Chamber finances as Keeper of the Privy Purse. His trusted position put him at the very centre of events, and he was one of the few witnesses at Henry's secret predawn marriage to Anne Boleyn.

The Privy Chamber

The private residence of the English monarch. Borrowed from the French court tradition it was staffed by Gentlemen or Gentlewomen of the Privy Chamber, who were close body servants in attendance on the king or queen. These servants were present at ceremonies and entertainments and carried royal authority, sometimes acting in the monarch's name.

However, such intimacy with the monarch could be extremely dangerous. Norris was a challenge to Thomas Cromwell, who sought to extend his own political influence, and he became caught up in the power struggle over access to the king that was inflamed by Henry's marriage to Anne. In 1536 he was executed for treason, having been convicted on trumped-up charges of having an adulterous affair with the queen.

THE HOUSE OF EASEMENT

Where one relieved oneself indicated a clear demarcation of power and political status at the Tudor court. While the king and other senior courtiers had their own personal toilets (and we know that these luxurious facilities were replicated in wealthy households around the kingdom, including those of Cardinal Wolsey and Bishop Fisher), lower-ranking courtiers would sit side by side in a row along a plank, in a location slightly removed from the court itself – known as 'the Great House of Easement'.

Such communal facilities were less commodious and much more malodorous. They were also non-flushing, which meant that they needed to be physically cleaned and scoured – a job undertaken by cleaners known as 'gong farmers', whose job was to dig out the 'gongs' or turds. At Hampton Court there was a more advanced system of plumbing, which channelled waste into a chute that passed into brick culverts and down into the Thames.

But the enforced sociability made such facilities an excellent location for scheming and plotting – as well as a perfect place into which to cast incriminating correspondence and documents. When in 1540 Viscount Lisle, Lord Deputy of Calais, was imprisoned for treason for clandestine correspondence with the exiled Catholic cardinal Reginald Pole, most of his family papers were seized by the state as evidence. However, a number of letters that the Lisles were keen to keep from the commissioners were 'cast into the jakes' (a slang word for toilets), to prevent them from being read and used in the trial. The Tudor toilet, therefore, could even become a repository for powerful knowledge.

·4·

ORANGES

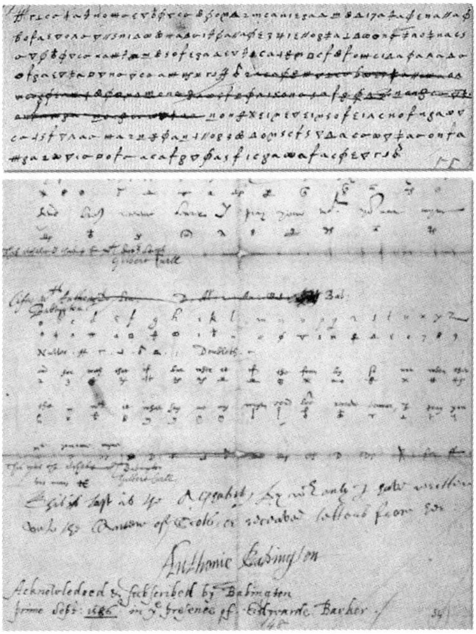

Anthony Babington postscript in cipher

Oranges were the tools of Tudor spies…

A VERSATILE TOOL FOR SUBTERFUGE

The orange was the fruit of choice for the spy and for those engaged in subterfuge in Tudor England. In his autobiography, the Jesuit priest John Gerard (1564–1637), who was persecuted for his religious beliefs and imprisoned and tortured for three years, provides an unusually detailed account of his use of the orange as a way of secretly communicating with the outside world.

Jesuits

Members of the Society of Jesus, a Catholic order. The society received papal approval in 1540, and Jesuits engaged in educational, charity and missionary work. They played an important role in the Counter-Reformation, and from 1580 onwards were sent to England as missionaries. Since Catholicism was banned during this period, Jesuits were hunted down and imprisoned.

Oranges, a valuable luxury food in Tudor England, were sent into the prison by Gerard's Catholic female supporters to sustain him during his hardships, and in his hands this fruit – as well as the paper it was wrapped in – was remarkably versatile.

The peel of the orange was used to form crosses and rosaries, which facilitated Gerard's Catholic practice and also made useful gifts to send to friends on the outside as tokens of political support – proof that he (and their cause) was still alive. The flesh of the fruit, a most desirable commodity, was used by Gerard to bribe the orange-loving warden to secure his cooperation in smuggling other items in and out. And the wrapping paper was used as a seemingly innocuous carrier of secret messages, all penned in the final component of the orange – its juice, which was used as an invisible ink that remained undetectable until treated with heat.

HIDDEN WRITING

The technique was simple. Gerard used charcoal and pencil to write visible messages, but there was invisible text between the lines too. As he later recalled: 'In the pencilled letter I confined myself to spiritual topics, but in the white spaces between the lines I gave detailed instructions to different friends of mine outside.'

Using the orange in this way, Gerard was able to communicate both with fellow prisoners and his supporters beyond the prison walls, all of whom knew to look for writing on the orange-wrappings. On receipt of the document they would rush to the nearest fireplace and hold the paper close to the heat to reveal its hidden message, which showed up as brownish stains.

Various invisible inks – including milk, onion juice, and even urine and beer – were widely used by Tudors conducting clandestine correspondences to transmit news, information and spiritual advice through underground networks. Their use became intricately linked with Elizabethan Catholics, who wanted to keep their banned religion a secret.

Oranges were preferable to lemons, as Gerard made clear in his own writings when he drew an important distinction between the different properties of their juices. 'I never used lemon or citron juice', he wrote, explaining that letters written in lemon juice could be read as easily with water as with heat, the difference being that, once the wet paper dried out, the lemon-juice message disappeared. The advantage was that a letter read in one place could then be taken on to another, but there was a major disadvantage for the would-be spy: the receiver never knew whether a letter had been intercepted or not. This was not the case with orange juice. As Gerard wrote, once the heat had brought the message 'out... it stays out', and thus 'a letter in orange juice cannot be delivered without the recipient knowing whether or not it has been read'.

A NETWORK FOR SPIES

Not only did the juice of the orange provide spies with the tools of their trade, but the trade in the oranges themselves provided a network for wide and fast international communication and transportation.

Oranges were a frequent item on the tables of Tudor elites and were enjoyed as an expensive delicacy. Trade in oranges from Spain and Portugal was healthy, and ships regularly sailed back and forth between southern Europe and England, laden with citrus cargo. Such was the volume of fruit in transit that, in 1581, a cargo of 20,000 oranges and 1,000 lemons reached Norwich. And these ships, which passed so regularly and freely between the warring Protestant England and Catholic Spain, were also used to carry agents, as well as their clandestine correspondence.

In early 1580, at the time of the Second Desmond Rebellion in Ireland, an intelligence letter from Spain sent by the soldier and administrator Sir Henry Radcliffe (1533–93) told of a small boat that had left the port of Bilbao 'loaded with oranges as if for merchandise', headed ostensibly for the French town of Nantes. But, undercover as a legitimate mercantile vessel, it instead made its way to Ireland.

The Desmond Rebellions

Two periods of armed conflict in Ireland in 1569-73 and 1579-83, during which the Elizabethan English state sought to extend its influence into Munster and clashed with the Earl of Desmond. The rebellions culminated in the decapitation of Gerald FitzGerald, last Earl of Desmond, which paved the way for the English colonization of Ireland.

Similarly, in 1598, at a time of high tension between Spain and England, the Secretary of State Sir Robert Cecil (1563–1612) was informed of a small vessel that had set sail from the southern Spanish port of Sanlúcar carrying letters for members of the Catholic underground. The vessel, named *Caval Volando* (*The Flying Horse*), was laden with a cargo of lemons and Seville oranges to throw the authorities off the scent of its true intent.

More news from Spain that found its way into the hands

of Secretary Cecil the following year reported a small barque travelling from the Spanish port of La Coruña – with the express purpose of gathering intelligence on English sea power – 'with a cargo of oranges and lemons to spy out the Queen's ships where they be, and in what readiness'.

·5·

THE MIRROR

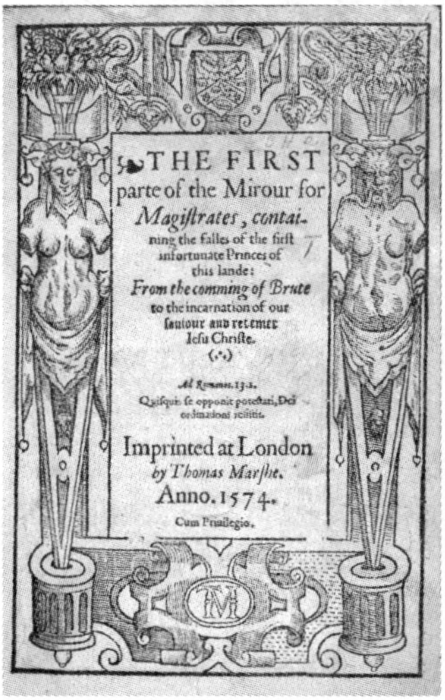

THE FIRST parte of the Mirour for *Magistrates, contai*ning the falles of the first infortunate Princes of this lande: *From the comming of Brute* to the incarnation of our sauiour and redemer Iesu Christe.

(.·.)

Ad Romanos. 13. 2.

Quisquis se opponit potestati, Dei ordinationi resistit.

Imprinted at London *by Thomas Marshe.* Anno. 1574.

Cum Priuilegio.

Title-page of *The Mirror for Magistrates* (London, 1574)

Tudor mirrors were all about giving advice…

LEARNING FROM MISTAKES

One of the most popular forms of Tudor publication was known as a 'Mirror', and one of the most significant was the *Mirror for Magistrates*. First published in 1559, the book was written to offer advice to magistrates and other people in positions of power – by reflecting on the deeds of famous individuals in order that readers might learn from their mistakes.

The idea was clever as well as important. In the form of a collection of poems, contributed by at least six different authors, the ghosts of nineteen famous people examined themselves in front of a mirror and offered warnings to those in the present by exploring the errors of their past. It was a literary work that 'used' history, rather than just recording it.

Subsequent editions included an increasing number of subjects. By 1610, no fewer than seventy-four famous lives had been explored through these reflections, including the Roman emperors Caesar, Tiberius and Caligula; the legendary British ruler King Arthur; the Anglo-Saxon rulers Alfred and Godwin; courtiers and clergymen like Cardinal Wolsey and Henry Percy, Earl of Northumberland; and the Plantagenet kings Edward IV and Richard II.

The lives of women were few and far between but some were discussed, including Queen Elstride – the concubine of the legendary Briton king Locrinus who was drowned by Queen Gwendoline the year before Christ – and Eleanor Cobham (c. 1400–52), Duchess of Gloucester, who was accused of practising witchcraft and sorcery and banished from the realm to live on the Isle of Man.

The *Mirror* followed in the footsteps of the fifteenth-century poet John Lydgate's *Fall of Princes* (1431–8), which was itself inspired by Giovanni Boccaccio's *De casibus virorum illustrium* (*Concerning the Falls of Illustrious Men*) of 1355–74, and it remained in print for over sixty years. In fact, so influential was this tradition of exemplary or advice literature that its ideas could be found in the works of contemporary dramatists, including literary giants such as Shakespeare.

THE KING'S PROTECTOR

This reflective form of advice was even offered to rulers, wrapped up in exemplars of how best to rule. When the mid-Tudor politician and fixer William, Lord Paget (1506–63) sought to counsel the autocratic Edward Seymour, Duke of Somerset – then protector of the young King Edward VI – on how to rule, he presented him with a 'schedule' of advice as a New Year's gift. In the accompanying letter, Paget explained that the schedule should act as a mirror or 'glass' into which His Grace should daily look, 'and by it you... shall so well apparel your self as eche man shall delight to behold you'.

Paget's mirror reflected to Somerset all the qualities necessary for just rulers. The advice included:

> Deliberate maturely in all things... Punish the disobedient according to their deserts... Reward the king's worthy

servants liberally and quickly... Keep your ministers about you uncorrupt.

By offering advice in this way – rather than direct criticism – Tudor officials could safely counsel rulers and high-ranking officials without incurring their wrath.

NAVIGATION

Another important advice-offering mirror was one produced specifically for sailors. In 1584, the Dutch cartographer Lucas Janszoon Waghener published *Spieghel der zeevaerdt* – later translated as *The Mariner's Mirrour.*

Sailors had traditionally navigated the world's oceans using a diverse collection of navigational aids, including charts, views of coastlines, written and oral sailing directions, depth soundings, landmarks, safe anchorages, and tables for finding the altitude of the sun. Now, and for the first time, Waghener brought these together into one volume. It became the single most important publication in the history of navigation.

It covered the entire coast of Europe, from Zeeland to Andalusia, and it was an instant success. Only a year after its publication, Lord Howard (1536–1624), then Lord High Admiral of England, persuaded the Privy Council to have it translated into English. The task was given to Anthony Ashley (1551–1628), a gifted and wise administrator and the Clerk of the Privy Council. Ashley not only translated the Dutch text but, where necessary, amended and improved it, and the first English edition was published in October 1588.

The Privy Council

Established by Thomas Cromwell in the 1530s, it became the main executive institution of government and was made up of influential men who were always on hand to advise the monarch. Its formation formalized the medieval tendency for royal government to draw advisers from among the most powerful men in the kingdom.

The Mariner's Mirrour appeared within three months of the defeat of the Spanish Armada, an event which, more than any other, made the English look long and hard at their maritime reflection. Importantly, one of the things that Ashley had seen was that there would be nothing to fear from 'exposing to the world the Draught of our Coasts'. Rather than national security, what Ashley was concerned with was a universal need to help mariners, a motivation that Samuel Pepys, later writing as secretary of the navy, admired as his 'zeal for this common good'.

A SPIRIT MIRROR

From time to time the Tudors even sought advice in actual mirrors. One of the most fascinating examples to survive is the 'spirit mirror' that was owned by the English magician, astrologer and mathematician John Dee (1527–1608), now in the collections of the British Museum.

Dee's mirror had its own deep history from which he drew power. The size of a small plate, it is made of obsidian – volcanic glass – and was brought to Europe at some point between 1527 and 1530. It came from Mexico, where such mirrors were used by Aztec priests to conjure visions and make prophecies, and was brought back to Europe by the Spanish conquistador Hernán Cortés, who subjugated Mexico between 1519 and 1521.

The Conquistadors

Professionally trained soldiers and explorers of the Spanish empire, who sailed and conquered territory outside of Europe from the late fifteenth to eighteenth centuries. Their explorations opened up trade routes in the new worlds of the Americas, Africa, Asia and the Pacific.

Dee held seances in both England and continental Europe, and part of his process involved consulting his spirit mirror, summoning angels into its reflective surface and conversing with them about the natural and supernatural worlds. Dee called these angels his 'scholemasters', because of what they taught him.

A great deal of information survives about these seances, and we know that Dee's angels were rather splendid. On one occasion a male angel appeared in the mirror dressed in a long purple robe, with a triple crown on his head and a red rod in his hand, and made the earth shake; soon after, Dee saw seven angels holding aloft a seven-pointed star made of copper, one of whom revealed feathers and a golden girdle beneath his robe.

Dee is believed to have been the inspiration behind

Shakespeare's magus Prospero in *The Tempest* (1610–11), whose character reveals an interesting contemporary concern over the use and abuse of magical powers. It is easy to see why he might have been the muse: on one occasion, Dee, who at the time was feeling some financial pressure from his creditors, asked an angel in his mirror for help finding hidden treasure.

·6·

THE GIFT

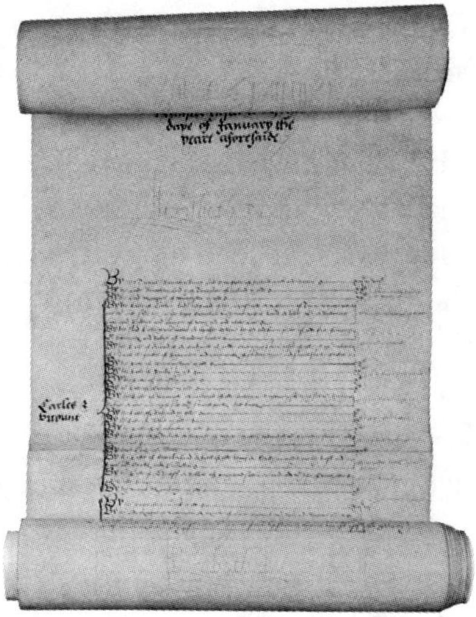

New Year's gift roll of Elizabeth I, 1 January 1585

Gifts made the Tudor world go round…

THE POWER OF EXCHANGE

The giving of gifts underpinned relationships of all kinds during the Tudor period. Gifts were an older form of exchange that rubbed alongside an emerging market economy system based on monetary payment for commodities. Whether it was a small pie or cheese that accompanied a request for a favour, a rare piece of fine jewellery, an original poem, or even a child placed in an aristocratic household, gifts were a lubricant that oiled the wheels of life during the sixteenth century. They quite literally made the Tudor world go round.

There was, however, no such thing as a free gift during the Tudor period, because there was always an expectation of receiving something in return. Sometimes this was unwelcome. In 1598, the English Secretary of State Sir Robert Cecil refused a gift of four pairs of Spanish gloves from Carlo Lanfranchi, an influential Italian merchant based in Antwerp, instead preferring to pay the bearer eight crowns a pair for them. In this way, a direct market exchange turned an intended gift into a purchased item – with the associated obligation discharged by the payment of money.

Being in somebody's debt was doubly problematic if you were the monarch, something that Elizabeth I knew all too well. Thus, during New Year 1585, when entertained as a guest by the nobleman Henry Seymour at Hanworth, Middlesex, the queen paid him fifty pounds in return for his gifts because she 'would not be in his debt'.

GIFT ROLLS

Perhaps the most lavish and ritualized form of gift-giving was the long-standing custom of presenting presents to the monarch on New Year's Day. This was a public ceremony that took place at the heart of the Tudor court, in the royal presence chamber. The Master of the Jewel House and his assistants carefully recorded gifts given to – and received from – high-ranking nobles and members of the royal household. These details were transferred to 'gift rolls', sheets of paper or membranes of vellum stuck or stitched together to form a single document measuring up to eleven feet in length, which was then rolled up and stored in the Jewel House.

The Jewel House

A vault in the Tower of London used to house the Crown Jewels, including jewellery, plate crowns and other regalia - with the exception of coronation regalia, which remained at Westminster Abbey until the seventeenth century.

One of the most intimate depictions of gift-giving at the court of Henry VIII survives in a 1538 letter from John Husee, the court agent of Lord Lisle, the Lord Deputy of Calais. In it, he writes: 'The King stood leaning against the cupboard, receiving all things; and Mr Tuke at the end of the same cupboard penning all things that were presented.' This was a remarkably personal political system that brought courtiers into direct contact with the monarch.

Gift rolls survive in archives around the world for nearly every year of the Tudor monarchy, and these fabulous documents reveal the nature of gift-giving at the very apex of society. While Henry VIII expected to receive gifts in gold, he also received more uncommon items, such as the 'sword the pommel and hilt gilt', 'brase of greyhounds' and 'book covered with green velvet' he was given in 1539.

Elizabeth I on the other hand preferred more original gifts, and the courtier Elizabeth Wingfield in 1585 counselled the Countess of Shrewsbury that gifts of money would be 'ill liked'. Of much greater prominence among gifts given to the queen were cloth, personal jewellery and trinkets. One of the most lavish was given to her in 1585 by her loyal spymaster and principal secretary Sir Francis Walsingham, who presented the queen with a sumptuously decorated 'French gown of russet satin flourished with leaves of silver bound about with a passamayne [lace] of Venice gold with pendant sleeves lined with cloth of silver'.

BEING IN FAVOUR

The gifts given in return at the New Year ceremony by both Henry and Elizabeth were much less elaborate and were normally gifts of gilt plate of varying weight and value according to the hierarchical status of the recipient. On occasion, however, both monarchs rewarded particular favourites more generously. In 1529, Henry VIII had his Groom of the Stool Henry Norris deliver to Cardinal Wolsey a 'great ryng of gold with a Turkkas for a token' as a sign of his personal favour when his chief minister was in political disgrace; while in 1572, Elizabeth grandly presented Walsingham with the painting *An Allegory of the Tudor Succession*, which bore the inscription:

'The Quene to Walsingham this tablet sente; Mark of her peoples and her owne contente.' These were intimate gifts from a monarch and signified high favour.

The presentation of gifts to the sovereign was imbued with political and social significance. Those in favour were permitted to exchange gifts with the monarch; those that were not in favour were barred from the court in general. The list of New Year's gifts throughout the Tudor period is thus a useful record of political standing and interpersonal relationships at court.

In 1532, during the significant tensions of Henry VIII's marriage to Catherine of Aragon, the imperial ambassador Eustace Chapuys reported that the king angrily declined the queen's gift of a gold cup at New Year, and sent no gift himself; his new love Anne Boleyn, however, received a room hung with gold cloth.

INTERNATIONAL DIPLOMACY

Gifts were also an important part of international diplomacy, and great care was taken by ambassadors as well as monarchs to offer well-chosen presents to foreign dignitaries. For example, both Henry VIII and Elizabeth I exchanged gifts with the Russian tsar Ivan the Terrible during their reigns.

Ivan the Terrible (1530–84)

Ivan IV was the Grand Prince of Moscow from 1533 to 1547, and then Tsar of All Russia until his death in 1584. He was an autocratic ruler who conquered vast lands, transforming the medieval Russian state into an empire, but at great cost to its people.

Among the royal portraits, armour and jewellery presented to the tsar were spectacularly lavish gifts of English and French silverware. In 1566, on a voyage to Russia on behalf of the Crown as a representative of the English-based Muscovy Trading Company, the traveller and writer Anthony Jenkinson brought with him royal gifts including 'a pair of candlesticks and two standing pots of silver'. While on a later embassy, Sir Jerome Horsey (c.1550–1626) conveyed from Elizabeth a menagerie of wild beasts including a white bull, twelve dogs wearing roses and collars, and two lions.

But in England, foreigners bearing gifts were often viewed with suspicion – not only for fear of what they might want in return, but also because it was seen as an empty gesture. In a series of considerations delivered before the 1559 Elizabethan parliament, one warned of Italian merchants above all others,

> for they in all tymes passe to go to and fro everywhere, and for themselves serve all princes at once, and with their perfumed gloves and wanton presents, and gold enough to boot if need be, work what they like.

And it was more that they sought to flatter with their promiscuous gifts and bribes; they were so distrusted it was said they would 'lick the fat even from our beards'.

A CURRENCY OF CHILDREN

The connection between gifts and human relationships was perhaps most acute when the gifts exchanged were humans themselves – in the form of children. Throughout the Tudor period, the practice of 'placing out' children – sending them to live in the households of others – was widespread, particularly among the aristocracy. In 1588, for example, the Countess of Rutland sent her eleven-year-old daughter Bridget Manners to live with the Countess of Bedford, who was to train her for service at court. She became a maid of honour in Elizabeth's service in 1589, a position that her uncle Roger Manners thought showed the queen's 'great and spetiall favor' towards her, which he considered was 'to the exceeding great comfort of all your frendes'. In other words, Bridget would be positioned to benefit her family and marry well.

It is striking how the language of gift-giving is used to describe this placing of children. The Elizabethan diarist Lady Margaret Hoby (1571–1633) recorded that one 'Mistress Bell' came 'to offer me the service of one of hir Daughters', and that her cousin Gates brought her his thirteen-year-old 'who, as he saied, he freely gave me'. In 1576 the Earl of Essex bequeathed his son Robert to Lord Burghley, 'upon the assured Confidence that your love to me shall dissend [descend] to my Childrenne' and that the good done to him would with honour and equity 'bind him with perpetual Friendship to you and to your House'.

Taking on the responsibility of these children, symbolic gifts in a political society, bound families together, extending their range of social and political contacts. Giving children in this way was political networking of the highest degree.

·7·

WINDOWS

Reformation iconoclasm of the Calvinists in the Netherlands, etching by Franz Hogenberg, 1566

Windows were all about dispute in Tudor Britain…

NOSY NEIGHBOURS

Windows in Tudor Britain were a source of air and light – but also of information and entertainment, and even temptation. For those looking *out*, windows offered a tantalizing, framed glimpse of the passing world; for those looking *in*, they offered a fascinating and addictive peep into someone else's private life.

European cities were blessed with more windows than ever before in this period, which led to major problems with privacy. The new prevalence of windows led to a rise in complaints, controversies and quarrels about 'annoying peeping in', and they also became a constant source of litigation throughout the period, as Tudor citizens – looking both out and in – reported on their neighbours, 'policing' their activities. In fact, peeping through window panes (or holes in walls) and 'bringing witnesses to look too' were acceptable forms of proof in canon law, the legal system made and enforced by the Catholic Church. In 1566, one Alice Pyckeringe charged Anne Parry with slander. Her case was strengthened by notes taken by a neighbour, Edward Godfrey, who sat in her window recording everything that left Parry's mouth as she railed against Alice. Another neighbour warned Parry, 'take heed what you say, for there is one in Pyckeringe's window that writeth all that you speak'.

The window was also a place from which to accuse and hurl

abuse: in 1579 in Boar's Head Alley, off Fleet Street, London, one Susan Symonds yelled at her neighbour Alice Amos with the choice words of the outraged and humiliated: 'Thou art a whore: And I saw my husband stand between thy legs and thou did put thy hand into his codpiece very rudely.'

Codpiece

Part of fashionable male attire during the fifteenth and sixteenth centuries, a codpiece (from the Middle English *cod*, meaning 'scrotum') was a pouch or flap that attached to the crotch area of men's trousers, accentuating the genitals.

SPIRITUAL PROBLEMS

For the Church, windows posed far deeper – even moral and spiritual – problems. In particular, the split between Catholic and Protestant beliefs was, curiously, reflected in their attitude towards windows. Catholics held true to Bible teachings, which saw only trouble in the idle gazing out of windows. It was thought to encourage lust and sin, a conviction that was reflected in church and monastic architecture, in which windows were obscured by coloured glazing, placed above the eye level or even entirely absent.

Protestants, however, embraced the window as a means of appreciating God's majesty – visible in the world he created – and also of displaying godly life and prosperity. The architecture of Hardwick Hall in Derbyshire, built between 1590 and 1597, took this to the extreme. Home of the Protestant courtier and aristocrat Elizabeth Talbot (1527–1608), Countess of Shrewsbury, this house was so spectacularly transparent that contemporaries quipped, 'Hardwick Hall, more glass than wall'. Designed by the reputed architect Robert Smythson, the new Hardwick was a complete contrast to what had stood before and was bathed in light.

Front entrance to Hardwick Hall at Hardwick in Derbyshire, UK

THE THREAT OF STAINED GLASS

Stained glass windows were a distinct source of anguish during the reigns of Henry VIII and Edward VI, when they became a target for Reformers in England. Traditionally, stained glass windows were made from lots of small pieces of coloured glass assembled using lead strips to form pictures and patterns, a method still in use today.

These included biblical scenes, images of saints, Christ and the Virgin Mary, as well as heraldic devices, fauna and flora. Across medieval Europe, such windows flourished as an art form in churches and cathedrals alike, and were a central part of traditional religious devotion. All this was to change, however, in the first half of the sixteenth century, as the Church in Rome and its religious rituals and practices came under attack.

For the Reformers in England, the images depicted in stained glass – particularly the saints and biblical figures – were viewed as superstitious, a form of idol worship. Attacks on stained glass windows occurred at the same time as other acts of iconoclasm, including the destruction of images, the whitewashing of Catholic art and the vandalism of statues of saints, many of whom lost their noses.

WIDESPREAD DESTRUCTION

The motivation for these attacks came from the very top. The Edwardian Injunctions of 1547 ordered the destruction of windows and whitewashing of walls that portrayed 'feigned miracles, pilgrimages, idolatry, and superstition', while in 1548 an order by the Privy Council ordered the removal from parish churches of all remaining images on the walls and elsewhere within the fabric of buildings.

The Edwardian Injunctions of 1547

These royal injunctions sought to reform religion and were essentially Cromwell's ones of 1538 with additions: the Bible was to be read in English; a number of 'superstitious' medieval practices were banned; and there was an order to destroy religious images that were considered accessories to idolatry.

In many churches, especially in southern and eastern parts of the country, widespread ruination was unleashed, with the mayor and aldermen of London receiving direct instructions from the council to paint over any images in stained glass that fell into the categories above. In 1548 in the parish church of Tidenham, Gloucestershire, the vicar himself broke the painted windows. Churchwardens' accounts from across the country indicate payments for repairing and reglazing windows with 'white glass'. The Norwich church of St John Bere Street paid nineteen shillings for the 'making of a glass window, wherein Thomas Becket was'.

While some 'hot' Protestants greeted the orders with a flurry of stone-throwing, others were more hesitant, since reglazing the resultant draughty churches was an expensive business. In certain instances, the glass was carefully taken down and put away, to be brought out and reinstalled during Mary's Catholic reign.

What people in different parts of the country did with their stained glass windows is a useful index of religious behaviour, and exposes fervent Protestantism alongside more traditional beliefs – as well as widespread acquiescence. Later, the revival of interest in stained glass in Elizabeth's reign was faced with the problem that by this point many of the traditional skills had been forgotten.

DEFENESTRATION

Throwing people out of windows was established in this period as a clear – if rather violent – political statement, and was even given a name: 'defenestration'. Most famous of all, the defenestration in 1618 of two imperial regents and their secretary in Prague was responsible for the start of the entire Thirty Years' War (1618–48), which tore all of Europe apart with more than three generations of conflict.

By then, defenestration was an established feature of violent protest in Europe. In 1572, Huguenot Protestants were butchered during the St Bartholomew's Day massacre, by methods including being hurled out of windows or off roofs. The last Scottish cardinal prior to the Reformation, David Beaton (c.1494–1546), Archbishop of St Andrews, was brutally murdered by Scottish lairds, his body mutilated and thrown out of the window to hang.

The St Bartholomew's Day massacre

In the summer of 1572, the wedding of Henry III, the young Huguenot King of Navarre, and Margaret, the King of France's Catholic sister, took place - a match intended to end the French Wars of Religion. But four days later the River Seine ran with blood as Huguenots were massacred, and the violence spread across France.

In Lincoln in 1586, a Privy Council messenger was beaten and threatened with defenestration by the local mayor's henchmen for what was considered interference in local politics; and in 1536, shortly after Henry VIII's split from the Catholic Church, several women attacked the local workmen as they set about dismantling the rood screen within St Nicholas' Priory in Exeter. Incensed by what they saw as sacrilegious behaviour, the terrifyingly fervent women chased one of the workmen up the tower and forced him to hurl himself from the window to escape – an act of auto-defenestration. Although the women were arrested, this curious episode also demonstrates one way in which ordinary women resisted the state imposition of Henry VIII's Reformation.

·8·

HATS

Portrait of William Parr, first Marquis of Northampton by Hans Holbein the Younger, c.1538–40

The Tudor hat was a secret code…

HIDING IN PLAIN SIGHT

In 1592, the English ambassador to Austria – and spy – Sir Henry Wotton arrived in Rome wearing a hat he had specifically chosen because he did not want to be recognized as a Protestant or Englishman.

He chose a black hat with 'a mighty blue feather'. He admitted that the hat 'though in itself… a slight matter' had three profound effects on those who viewed it. First, that there was no chance that he was an Englishman; second, that he was considered 'as light in my mind as in my apparel' and therefore of no threat; and third, that it would be impossible for such a man to want to be ignored. Wotton the spy was, in effect, hiding in plain sight by wearing a hat that he knew would make him 'famous through Rome in a few days'.

This wonderful example opens up a window into the Tudor world, in which one's hat could be a symbol of an impressive variety of things: one's profession, social status, age, wealth, nationality, education and political or religious identity. The popular Elizabethan song 'Ballad of the Caps' spells out some of the social nuances and meanings of Tudor headwear:

> The Monmouth-cap, the saylors thrum,
> And that wherein the tradesmen come;
> The physic, lawe, the cap divine,
> And that which crowns the muses nine;

The cap that fools do countenance,
The goodly cap of maintenance,
And any cap, whate're it bee,
Is still the sign of some degree.

RARE SURVIVALS

Hats were worn by all but the very poorest in Tudor society, and remarkably a number of examples owned by a wide variety of people – men, women, children, young and old, rich and poor – survive. Most of them were discovered by chance during archaeological excavations or were preserved for their sartorial qualities in private collections – and later in museums – and they are special indeed.

Some of the most fascinating, for their widespread use and manufacture, are the felt caps such as those in the collections of the Museum of London, which were commonly made from fur pelts. A single piece of fabric was shaped over a wooden block with the use of heat and moisture, to form an individual hat. These were an affordable alternative to the velvet caps of the aristocracy.

More ubiquitous still were woollen hats, and the wearing of them was not just a matter of fashion. In 1571, during Elizabeth's reign, an Act of Parliament was passed that required anyone above six years of age, 'excepting maids, ladies, gentlewomen' and noble Englishmen, to wear a woollen hat on Sundays and holidays – but not just any wool. The law required it to be *English* wool, and the hats themselves were to be 'only dressed and finished by some of the trade of cappers'. Those caught without them were fined three shillings and four pence per day.

The popularity of these low-status woollen caps shows how most English people followed such laws. It also highlights the presence of the English state in support of the English wool trade and cap-making industry, even if the law proved unworkable and was repealed in 1597.

Cappers

The medieval hat trade was complicated. The ordinances of the craft of cappers were made in 1270, setting out rules and regulations for cap-making. They went on to gain royal approval in 1318 from Edward II. Cappers were distinct from 'Hatters', though it remains unclear exactly how and why they were different, and both trades were different to the 'Hurers' who were responsible for the 'thicking' process of both hats and caps (i.e. making them shaggy or bristly). In the early sixteenth century, the three trades merged to form the Company of Merchant Haberdashers.

But even these most basic of hats reveal a firework of taste and fashion. They could be simple skull caps or fitted with ear flaps; they could be brimmed – even with multiple brims; they could be decorated with slashes, ribbons or feathers; they could be dyed a variety of colours using woad (blue), weld (yellow) and madder (rose); and they could also be augmented with a wide range of jewellery – we now know that Tudor men decorated their clothes with jewellery as much as the women did.

NIGHT FASHION

So much for the day, but what of the night? Nightcaps have been lost to history, but in the draughty homes of the Tudor period they were very popular. They spoke as much of relaxation and domesticity as they did of sleep: not only were they worn in bed for warmth as one might assume, but they were also worn around the house in the evening, a visible symbol that the working day had ended. This meant that nightcaps not only appeared in the privacy of the bedroom but in the more public rooms of a dwelling, regardless of the presence of guests. They were, therefore, another valuable tool in the display of wealth, taste or status.

A particularly magnificent example, thought to have belonged to the ill-fated Sir Thomas More, survives in the collections of Stonyhurst College, a Catholic school founded in 1593. A linen cap, it is embroidered beautifully with silk and silver-gilt thread, the patterns a knot-garden of so many strawberries and roses – images connected with beauty and fertility.

Sir Thomas More (1478–1535)

One of the most important early Tudor statesmen, More was secretary and adviser to Henry VIII and was the Lord High Chancellor of England from 1529 to 1532. He failed to support Henry in his divorce from Catherine of Aragon and the split from the Church in Rome, and was subsequently beheaded for treason in 1535. He wrote a number of important works, including *Utopia* (1516).

HATS AND MEANING

In addition to style and aesthetic taste, the manner in which people wore hats was telling. The angle at which hats were worn – and such angles are recorded in paintings from the period – was taken as a personal statement. The courtier poet Sir Thomas Wyatt, for example, preferred to have his portrait painted wearing his hat at a jaunty angle, rather than flat on his head in the style of more conservative sitters such as Thomas Cromwell or Sir Thomas More, both of whom were depicted by the court artist Hans Holbein in black felt caps typical of those worn by lawyers.

Ornaments worn in hats were also coded, and communicated meanings that were more personalized – expressing an individual's learning, religious views and even marital status. A 1536 portrait of Henry VIII depicts him in a black velvet bonnet with a badge of the Virgin Mary upon it. Despite it being painted at the start of the Dissolution of the Monasteries, his choice hints at more conservative religious convictions.

To display one of Queen Elizabeth I's gloves on your hat was a sign of being favoured. The queen's champion George Clifford, 3rd Earl of Cumberland, was portrayed in a full-length portrait with a single glove in his hat. Wearing a hat that was part of the monarch's livery also signalled allegiance to the Crown, and twice a year certain groups of Henry VIII's servants were chosen to be particularly favoured and were presented with headwear as part of their liveried uniform.

Hat etiquette – when to remove, go bare-headed or doff – tells us much about social hierarchies in Tudor England. In general terms, men were more likely to be required to remove hats than women, while men of lower social standing were expected to doff hats in the presence of men or women of

Portrait miniature of George Clifford, 3rd Earl of Cumberland
by Nicholas Hilliard, c.1590

higher status, as a gesture of deference. An Italian visitor at the court of Henry VII observed that courtiers showed 'the incredible courtesy of remaining with their heads uncovered with an admiral grace, whilst they talk to each other'. In 1526, the Eltham Ordinances required men to doff their caps in the presence chamber at court even in the absence of the king.

What people did with hats also depended on where they were, and not just in whose presence they were in. Hats were routinely worn indoors, but rules stipulated that bell-ringers entering the belfry could be fined for failing to remove their hats (as well as their gloves and spurs).

·9·

BONES

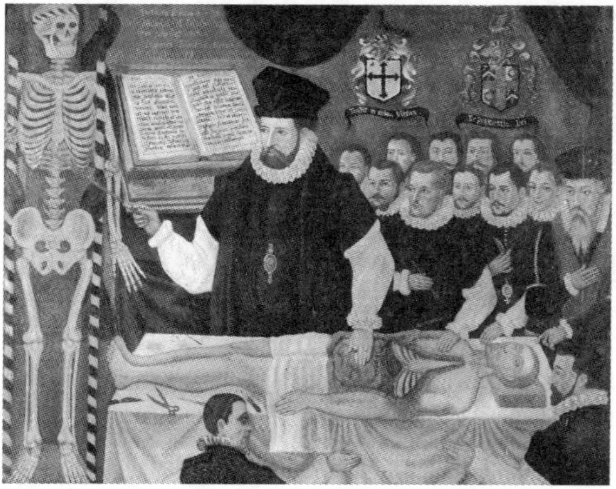

Portrait of John Banister delivering an anatomical lecture at the Barber-Surgeons' Hall, London. c.1580

Bones were a source of conflict in Tudor Britain...

RELICS

Bones were simply everywhere in Tudor England – and they were at the heart of a major conflict between warring sides. Indeed, bones as relics were an important battleground for the religious tensions between the Catholic world and Protestant Reformers throughout Europe.

Within the late medieval Church, the physical remains or personal effects of dead saints were venerated, including their bones. Not only was this a form of remembrance of religious heroes and heroines, but also it was felt that – by visiting, kissing, touching or even licking the bones – the worshipper could find divine protection or even achieve intercession with God himself.

In the early Tudor period, this belief in the power of bone relics was widespread and little questioned. They were a central part of traditional religion, so much so that almost every shrine or holy place had its own set of relics. Among the most famous were the bones of Thomas Becket, housed at Canterbury Cathedral. The Dutch theologian Desiderius Erasmus (1466–1536) recalled being shown the martyr's skull: 'the top of the cranium is bared for kissing, the rest covered with silver'.

Thomas Becket (1119–70)

Archbishop of Canterbury from 1162 to 1170, he was assassinated by knights in Canterbury Cathedral because of his disagreement with the king, Henry II, over the power of the Church.

There was even a thriving trade in relics of all sorts throughout the sixteenth century. In October 1512, the holy man Peter de Silva brought with him to England – with the support of the Bishop of Famagusta in Cyprus – various relics, including 'some of the bones of St Helena', 'part of Christ's sponge' and a piece of 'the cloth with which St Jerome wiped his wounds'.

CHURCH CONFLICT

These traditional beliefs and practices brought the late medieval Church into conflict with Reformers, both within and outside of the Church of Rome. For Reformers, the veneration of relics such as bones was deemed idolatrous. Erasmus was critical in his *A Dialoge or communication…* (1540) of what he saw as the superstitious worship of 'bones, heads, jaws, arms, coats, caps, hats, shoes, mitres, slippers, saddles, rings, beads, girdles, bowls, bells, noses, gloves, toys, tapers, candles, boots'.

Charges of profiteering from relics were also rife among the Reformers, who sought to discredit the irreligious use of 'rotten bones that be called relics'. During the campaign to dissolve the monasteries, which were treasure troves of bones, the commissioners charged with visiting religious houses catalogued, in a humiliating way, the illusory use of relics.

At Bury St Edmunds in 1536 it was recorded that 'John Melford, the Abbot, delights in the company of women and in sumptuous banquets' and that among the 'vain and fictitious relics' were the bones of St Botulph. It was noted that 'it is the custom whenever rain is wanted to carry about in processions the shrine containing the bones of St Botulph, in the hope that rain will come the sooner'.

St Botulph (c.610–80)

An English abbot trained in Gaul and sent back to establish the Benedictine Order in England, he was one of the most important Christian missionaries of the seventh century and the patron saint of travellers. He built a monastery in Iken, Suffolk, that was destroyed in a Viking attack.

The exposing of medieval relics as forgeries and fakes was part of Henry VIII's propaganda war against the Church of Rome, and many were either smashed or burned on the spot. We know, for example, that the relics of the twelfth-century St Hugh of Lincoln were destroyed during Henry's reign.

MILITARY CONFLICT

Broken bones were also the result of new and revolutionary modes of warfare. Gunpowder had been used in European armies since the first half of the thirteenth century, but it was during the Tudor period that the scale and number of firearms really exploded. This in turn multiplied the number of complex wounds that needed to be dealt with, both on the battlefield and – because guns became portable and thus concealable in this period – on the streets of European cities and ports.

For example, an Elizabethan merchant from London, Thomas Gore, was shot by a Dutch soldier in the hand and upper part of his arm in Flushing, suffering a particularly nasty wound that could only have been caused by a lead ball propelled at high velocity. According to a report, not only was his arm broken, but the ball 'also brake that bone in many pieces, which did rent and tear the muscles, sinews, veins, and arteries'.

SURGERY

Techniques for mending and setting breaks and fractures were well-developed by the Tudor period, which saw a growing professionalism among physicians and surgeons. In 1540 the Worshipful Company of Barber Surgeons received a royal charter, which allowed its members to set broken bones, pull rotten teeth and perform simple surgery.

The most advanced Tudor techniques in bone surgery were described in the textbook *A Prooued Practise for All Young Chirurgians* (1588) by William Clowes, chief surgeon of the English fleet during the Armada. In it, he details how to deal with 'burnings with gunpowder, and woundes made with gunshot, sword, halbard, pyke, launce', and outlines ample examples of setting broken bones. In one section, entitled 'The manner and order of the taking or cutting off a mortified & corrupt leg or arme', Clowes describes the best procedure for amputation. With no anaesthetic, it was key to have a sharp saw and to work with 'a stedy and quick hand' to cut the flesh around the bones, and then 'with a light hand speedily sawe it off'. Wounds were then cauterized with heat to stem the bleeding.

We know in great detail what tools Tudor surgeons had to hand because, in 1982, a barber surgeon's wooden medical chest was raised intact with the wreck of the *Mary Rose*, which sank off Portsmouth in 1545. It contained around sixty different objects relating to the barber surgeon's practice, including a syringe, bowls, razors, an ear scoop for removing earwax and an enema tube, as well as all manner of surgical tools and medicaments necessary for mending fractures, setting bones and treating disease.

The bones found on the wreck were also very informative: some of the sailors were fighting fit and healthy and well-fed, while others revealed vitamin deficiency which would have led to rickets or scurvy. There was also evidence of healed fractures, several broken noses and an arrow wound, while fused vertebrae showed the crew were used to heavy lifting on board – an essential part of naval conflict in this period, as sails had to be hoisted high, anchors raised, cannon positioned and cargo stowed.

MUNICIPAL BONESETTER

On the whole, though, the plight of wounded soldiers and sailors throughout Elizabeth's wars in Europe and Ireland was not a happy one. While the Tudor state imposed a policy of repatriation of maimed men, many of those who were transported home died from their wounds en route, either from disease or as a result of lack of adequate nourishment. The Lord High Treasurer William Burghley did not help matters by wilfully starving troops of the money needed to pay for their survival and sustenance.

When injured soldiers and sailors returned from the wars, they could become something of a financial burden on the state. Efforts were made by local authorities to cater for their needs – to the benefit of the general populace. In 1574, the City of Norwich appointed a municipal bonesetter at an annual salary of four pounds: one Richard Durrant, 'a man very skilful in bone-setting', who was responsible 'for the relief of some as shall fortune by misfortune to have their legs, arms, or the bones of other parts of their limbs to be broken'.

·10·

LISTS

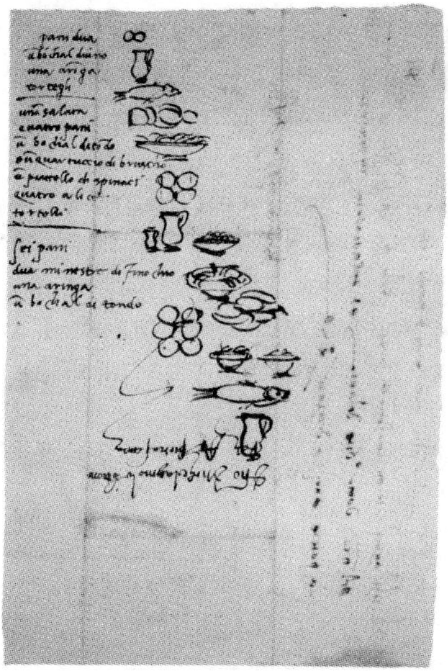

Shopping list of Michelangelo (1475–1564)

Lists are a window into the world of Tudor decision-making…

THE DEATH OF A LOVED ONE

In January 1588, Richard Rogers (1551–1618), the non-conformist lecturer at Wethersfield in Essex, faced a life-changing decision. His pregnant wife, who was near to delivery, was in great pain and very likely to die. Rogers, therefore, had to contemplate a life without her, as well as the prospect of remarrying.

The son of a Chelmsford carpenter, Rogers had attended Christ's College before completing an MA at Caius College. The religious training he received at university prepared him for whatever life had to throw at him. So he opened his spiritual journal and drew up a list as a way of preparing himself for the sad eventuality of the passing of his beloved wife – seeing, as he put it, 'many likelihoods of our separation':

- First, the fear of marrying again, dangerous as 2nd marriages are.
- Want of it in the mean while.
- Forgoing so fit a companion for religion, housewifery, and other comforts.
- Loss and decay in substance.
- Care of household matters cast on me.
- Neglect of study.
- Care and looking after children.
- Forgoing our boarders.
- Fear of losing friendship among her kindred.

Caius College

One of the oldest and largest colleges of the University of Cambridge, it has produced fourteen Nobel Prize winners. Famous fellows include: Sir James Chadwick (1891–1974), discoverer of the neutron; Sir Howard Florey (1898–1968), co-discoverer of penicillin; Francis Crick (1916–2004), co-discoverer of the structure of DNA; and Stephen Hawking (1942–2018).

His list was a way of making the infinite and uncertain comprehensible: by writing his thoughts down, his nameless fear became a practical problem to be addressed. Rogers's pondering reveals his anxieties over remarriage and the numerous disadvantages to a Tudor man of being without a spouse – from the lack of conjugal sex (no. 2 on the list) to not having a helper to take care of the household and children. His concerns also reveal the practical nature of Tudor marriage, and the balanced demarcation of duties between husband and wife. By reading this list, we are able to eavesdrop on some of the most intimate decisions of a private Tudor life.

A KING'S MINISTER

At a less ordinary level, the practice of writing lists also reveals the dynamics of decision-making at the very heart of Tudor politics. One of the most inveterate list-makers of the period was Thomas Cromwell, Henry VIII's chief minister. The son of a blacksmith, throughout the 1530s he accrued remarkable power as Principal Secretary, Chancellor of the Exchequer and Lord Privy Seal. Through these offices and others, Cromwell enforced the king's religious policies and prosecuted those who refused to accept them. He also oversaw broader domestic and foreign policy, and so a welter of affairs crossed his desk.

This meant that Cromwell dealt with high-profile matters of state alongside the mundane matters that comprised so much of the daily grind of government office. As a way of managing the day-to-day burdens of his enormous political role, he drew up lists or 'remembrances', hundreds of which survive in the National Archives in London. Typical of these Cromwellian lists is a memorandum dated 1533 which bears the title 'Special remembrances to be done with the King's Highness'. The document is an illuminating snapshot of the varied and hugely complex work that Cromwell undertook:

- First, to speak with the King touching the duke of Bayver's ambassador for his depechee [departure], and what shall be the effect of the King's letters, and what gifts he will give him.
- To speak with the King for the depechee of the gentleman of Polonia...
- To declare to the King the saying of Augustine touching the French ambassador.
- Of the answer of my lord of London for the benefice of Fulham.
- Touching friar Reysbye's examination…
- To know what way the King will take with all the said malefactors...
- For signing the ambassador of France's passports.
- To cause George to seek the copy of Dr. Benette's benefices, and to move the King to give them…

- To remember such as be taken for counterfeiting money, said to be done in Rouen and Normandy...
- To remember the signature of my warrants for such money as I have disbursed of the King...
- To speak to the Lord Chancellor for an injunction for Silvester Darius.
- To remember for money for Mr. Pattes, the King's ambassador in Spain.

This extract is from a document which extends to over three sides, and shows Cromwell discussing with the king matters of religious and diplomatic policy while also issuing warrants and signing letters.

A FORTUNE TELLER

Notable in the Cromwell document is the way in which he handled the fallout from the prophecies of the Nun of Kent, a young woman named Elizabeth Barton who foretold of Henry VIII's death should he remarry after he divorced Catherine of Aragon.

Elizabeth Barton (1506–34)

An English Catholic nun from a poor background in Kent who became famous for her prophecies, so much so that in 1528 she was summoned to meet Henry VIII himself - but she was executed when her visions began to oppose his royal supremacy. Barton is the only woman in history to have her head put on a spike on London Bridge.

The Franciscan friar Richard Risby ('friar Reysbye') was one of those implicated in the affair, and this list shows Cromwell's involvement in his examination and his intention to apply Henry's ruling to the rest of the malefactors who did not accept the king's religious policy and marriage. Elizabeth Barton was hanged for treason, along with Risby and six others.

Another surviving example of Cromwell's remembrances includes a note 'to Remembre the Auncyent Cronycle of Magna Carta and how *libera sit* Cam into the Statute'. Although undated, it is highly likely that this can be linked to his involvement in the trial of Thomas More (1478–1535), since he used this very clause of Magna Carta against the Lord Chancellor – who refused to swear the Oath of Supremacy to Henry VIII, a refusal that cost him his head.

A SPY'S LIST

One of the most fascinating Tudor lists in British archives is a captured one: an inventory of the entire Spanish Armada. This inventory somehow came into the possession of Sir Francis Walsingham, Elizabeth's spymaster, who had it translated from the Spanish. The list is interesting because we know that Walsingham had it in his hands on 18 May 1588, two months and a day before the Armada was first sighted from Plymouth. It is an important reminder that the English understanding of the threat posed by the Armada was characterized by a curious mixture of knowledge and ignorance. They knew in great detail about the preparations being made by the Spaniards, but at the same time did not know about the reality on the ground: in spite of what was written on this list, the Spanish fleet was suffering from an inadequate supply of shot, gunpowder, food, sailors and soldiers.

The Spanish Armada

An invasion force of some 130 Spanish ships that set sail in May 1588 under the command of the Duke of Medina Sidonia. The ships were carrying an army with the aim of overthrowing Elizabeth I, the Protestant Queen of England. The Armada was harried and defeated by English naval forces, and forced to return home in September 1588.

Nevertheless, the list made the English aware of just how far advanced the Spanish preparations were, and it influenced them to take positive action. Just twelve days after Walsingham got hold of the inventory, the English sailed to Lisbon in an attempt to destroy the Armada before it could venture out, but they were blown back by foul winds. Two further attempts also failed in the subsequent weeks. It meant that the English were forced simply to watch and wait for their enemy.

The list is interesting for another reason: at the foot of a long line of lengthy Spanish names such as Don Franco de Bonadelia, Don Alonso Lucan and Don Franco de Toledo, the English translator becomes so infuriated he scribbles:

> A pox upon them all, if they come into England I trust you will Cristen them ere they retourne, that their names may be easier to write. They be but dor beggars all, that goe to stele and become rich. Never take noe prisoners: hang them for ransom!

·11·

FIRE

John Foxe, *Acts and Monuments*: Martyrdom of Alexander Gouch and Alice Driver, 1558

The Tudor state communicated using fire…

DANGER BEACONS

At a time when most of the men and women in the country were illiterate, the Tudor state communicated using fire. This included the lighting of fires as a visual warning of imminent danger. During the sixteenth century, the country was linked by beacons, which were used to spread the news of an enemy fleet or a threatened invasion, as well as a summons to arms for the local militia. Once lit, a chain of beacons reached far and wide, deep into the countryside; a series of flaming signals that saw fire bouncing from hilltop to hilltop.

Instructions survive detailing the lighting and use of these beacons from the early years of Elizabeth's reign. Local militias were responsible for maintaining, fuelling and keeping watch over the beacons, which were grouped in threes along the coast and in pairs inland. During the day they were manned by two men, with three taking over at night – all of whom had to be 'an honest householder' over the age of thirty.

The beacons sent communications via an agreed pattern of signals. According to a 1558 letter circulated to the Justices of the Peace for Holderness and other parts of the East Riding of Yorkshire, one beacon should be lit by the coastal watchmen if any ships acted suspiciously; two if a 'great number of ships' gave 'vehement suspicion to be enemies'; and all three if they 'land to invade', which would activate the mobilization of the militia.

THE SPANISH ARMADA

Most famously, during the years before the Spanish Armada of 1588 when the Spanish invasion threat was at its height, the county of Devon had a network of some eighty-nine beacons set up at strategic points along the coastline and inland, including a beacon at the key vantage point of Plymouth Hoe. This speaks of Devon's significance as a pivotal maritime county and front line in the maritime war with Spain; the number of beacons here was higher than anywhere else in England. By comparison, even other coastal counties had far fewer, with Kent mustering forty-three beacons, and Hampshire and Sussex with twenty-four each.

What is perhaps less well known, however, is that almost no beacons were lit to warn of the Spanish Armada, contrary to popular assumption. It was believed that the lighting of beacons was likely to induce a sense of unwanted panic among the population during the heightened tensions of the 1580s, and therefore strict instructions were put in place that beacons were only to be lit with the express permission of the Lord Lieutenant – a measure of last resort.

HERETICS

Flames were a key part of the propaganda techniques employed by the Tudor state for combating sedition, heresy and blasphemy. Set-piece burnings at key sites in the Tudor capital of London, as well as at the universities of Oxford and Cambridge, were central to the ways in which Tudor monarchs flexed their political muscle.

Most famously, perhaps, the Tudor government communicated its displeasure by burning people accused of different types of crimes. The Tudors were not unique in this – there is a recorded burning for heresy in 1222 (during the reign of Henry III), and there were Acts of Parliament in 1382 (Richard II), 1401 (Henry IV) and 1414 (Henry V) that gave statutory authority for burning heretics. But historians are certain that the practice died out, to be reintroduced by the first Tudor king, Henry VII.

Interest in burning as a form of punishment and means of communicating belief and policy centred around the ancient Roman Catholic idea that, by killing without spilling blood, the process cleansed the soul at the same time as depriving the victim of a body to take into the next life – the most severe form of punishment. Burning, therefore, was the execution of choice for those whose souls were particularly corrupt. In mainland Europe it was primarily used for those accused of witchcraft, but in England witchcraft was a felony and therefore those accused of it were hanged.

In England, burning was used for women accused of treason; men were hanged, drawn and quartered, although parts of them were burned. The mid-Tudor diarist Henry Machyn recorded the public execution for treason of the rebel Sir Thomas Wyatt, who, on 11 April 1554, was beheaded at Tower Hill for his part in the Wyatt Rebellion. He was then 'quartered on the scaffold and his bowels and his members [genitals] burned beside the scaffold there'. His head and four quarters were 'put into a basket' and carted 'to Newgate to be parboiled'.

The Wyatt Rebellion of 1554

An anti-Catholic uprising that took place in England in the early years of Mary I's reign, designed to replace her on the throne with Elizabeth. Named after one of its leaders - Thomas Wyatt, a nobleman from Kent - it was poorly planned and executed, and thus failed miserably. Wyatt was the only one of the leaders to succeed in raising an army.

Most commonly, however, burning was used for those of either sex who were accused of heresy. During the reign of Henry VII, twenty-four heretics were burned; there were eighty-one during that of Henry VIII; and just two in the six years of Edward VI's reign. Mary was the one to really embrace the bonfires. During the five-year reign of this Catholic monarch, almost 300 men and women were burned for being Protestants (though this was nothing compared to what went on in Catholic Spain, where during the Inquisition an estimated 150,000 people were persecuted and several thousand executed). Elizabeth was not so fond. Although she ordered the deaths of many people, they tended to be hanged or beheaded rather than burned. Just four heretics were burned during Elizabeth's forty-four-year reign.

During the Tudor period, burnings took place in more than sixty towns in England; it was a very public and very popular spectacle. Everyone in Tudor England would have been familiar with it as a punishment, and thousands would have personally witnessed the punishment flames of the Tudor state. The prominent English martyrologist John Foxe (1516–87) captured in printed form the horrors of these

Protestant burnings in his *Actes and Monuments* (1563). This volume – popularly known as *Foxe's Book of Martyrs* – included gruesome woodcuts depicting the burnings of ordinary men and women, as well as those of well-known public figures such as the former Archbishop of Canterbury Thomas Cranmer, who is shown asking God to receive his spirit as the flames lick over his body. Such striking visual propagandist images meant the message of fire was communicated to the English nation, literate or not.

Actes and Monuments (1563)

John Foxe's polemical account of the suffering of Protestant martyrs, published early in the reign of Elizabeth I. One of the most important histories created in the early modern period, at the time it was the largest publishing project ever undertaken in England.

BOOK-BURNING

It was not just people that the Tudors burned, however; they also burned books. This public spectacle was all part of Tudor censorship, through which the state sought to control communication.

In May 1521, the bishop of Rochester, John Fisher, preached against heresy in the churchyard of St Paul's Cathedral. During his sermon various books by the German reformer Martin Luther were cast into the fire and burned. All of this was performed before Cardinal Wolsey and the assembled imperial and papal ambassadors, as a symbol of English resistance to reformist teachings and loyalty at this stage to the Roman Catholic Church.

There were some inventive punishments for owning banned books. In 1530, the London merchant Thomas Sommers was caught with illegal English translations of the Gospels. He was made to ride in a procession through London, from the Tower to Cheapside, with others who had also been caught with illegal tomes. They were all made to 'wear' the books by tying them around themselves – a sort of penitent costume. Sommers laced his books together and wore them with the leaves open as a type of collar.

Occasionally, books and people were even burned together. In Mary I's reign, the corpses of two leading theologians of the Reformation, Paul Fagius and Martin Bucer – both of whom had died several years previously – were exhumed, condemned as heretics, and then set alight in the marketplace at Cambridge along with 'a cart load of books'. A woodcut of this episode in Foxe's *Actes and Monuments* is one of only a few contemporary illustrations of the burning of books. Much like the burning of people, this type of punishment significantly declined during the reign of Elizabeth I.

·12·

EYES

Elizabeth I's 'Rainbow Portrait', c.1600, Hatfield House

Eyes in Tudor England were all about loyalty…

BIG BROTHER

Eyes were everywhere in Tudor England. The state and its informants were watching and waiting for malefactors to reveal themselves – for the many political and religious opponents of the Tudor regime to do or say the wrong thing.

During the reign of Henry VIII the treason laws were tightened after the split from Rome, to include treason by spoken word as well as by deed or writing. While sixteenth-century England was far from the kind of totalitarian states seen in twentieth-century Europe, there was still a sense that Big Brother was watching.

The image of the eyes of the state closely monitoring its subjects, borders and enemies abroad is strikingly depicted in the famous 'Rainbow Portrait' of Elizabeth I at Hatfield House.

Hatfield House

Built by Robert Cecil, 1st Earl of Salisbury, for the entertaining of royalty, this country house in Hertfordshire was visited by James I in 1611. Cecil died a year after it was completed but Hatfield has remained in the Cecil family ever since. It is now one of the most important surviving Jacobean houses, as well as a treasure trove of Tudor and Jacobean art.

It bears the motto *Non sine sole iris* ('No rainbow without the sun'), reinforcing the wisdom and the power of the queen to uphold peace – represented by the rainbow that she holds. Look closely, however, and you will see that the sleeves of her dress are decorated with tiny embroidered eyes (and ears), which depict the all-seeing and all-hearing power of the monarchy.

Close-up of the eyes and ears represented in Elizabeth's 'Rainbow Portrait'

This was not empty symbolism. Informants (or 'watchers') were vigilant throughout the land, especially in times of national crisis such as those years after the Spanish Armada when the threat of invasion was higher than ever and Elizabeth – an ageing and childless monarch – remained on the throne. Anxiety was everywhere at this time. Writing in October 1596 to the Earl of Essex, the Cambridge scholar Matthias Holmes rejoiced at the earl's fame abroad and favour with the queen but exhorted him 'to be careful to take foreign intelligences' since 'All men's eyes are upon you now at home and abroad, and your eyes must be upon all men, spying out home treasons and foreign plots.'

A GOGGLE-EYED WHORE

Throughout the Tudor period, prying eyes monitored public places such as the alehouse, and contemporary court records are full of reports from informants who witnessed misdeeds or overheard treasonable words: the spying eye in Tudor England was very closely related to the eavesdropping ear.

In 1534, in the aftermath of Henry VIII's divorce from Catherine of Aragon, a Suffolk woman named Margaret Chaunseler was witnessed calling Henry VIII's new wife, Anne Boleyn, 'a naughty whore' and 'a goggle-eyed whore' and saying 'God save queen Catherine'. In her defence, Margaret claimed that these words had been uttered while she was drunk, that the 'evil spirit did cause her to speak them', and that she was very penitent for her offences. Whether she meant these words or not, they nonetheless represent an undercurrent of criticism and opposition to the Tudor rule throughout the long sixteenth century.

Watchful eyes made sure that such sentiments did not overflow into outright rebellion, however. The punishments for seditious speech, political gossip and criticizing one's social superiors were extreme. They included the nailing, ripping, cropping and chopping off of ears, the slitting of nostrils, the branding of cheeks and foreheads with the letters 'F' and 'A' (for 'false accuser'), boring holes through tongues with a hot iron, and on rare occasions the 'putting out' of eyes.

BLINDING

The putting out of eyes has been a form of punishment in different cultures throughout history, and was well known – though perhaps little practised – in the Tudor age. Most famously it was represented on stage in Shakespeare's play *King Lear* (1608), where the Duke of Gloucester has his eyes put out for alleged treason.

Actual accounts of it happening in the period are scarce – and there are none of it occurring in England – but in a letter to Sir Francis Walsingham dated 1589, the Elizabethan ambassador in Constantinople, Edward Barton, wrote of a Greek friar caught preaching Christianity to the Turks who was condemned to an agonizing death, including having his eyes put out. He was raised by cord and pulley and dropped 'upon a sharp iron hook', then left there to hang. The friar carried on preaching until his angry punishers cut out his tongue and cut off his nose, ears and fingers, before putting out his eyes and, finally, stoning him. He survived this ordeal, we are told, for five hours.

SOUL-SEARCHING

The eyes were also connected to treason because it was believed that, of all the facial features, they marked a person's character: for the Tudors, eyes were a window into the soul.

Dangerous or devious sorts were often described as having shifty or distrustful eyes. An undated report on how to recognize Catholic priests travelling into England from the continent during Elizabeth's reign describes a twenty-two-year-old man named Griffin who was prone to keeping his head down, with very dark eyes, one of which was 'goggled' – a roving or bulging eye that may have signified distrustfulness.

Eyes could also reveal repentance, especially when filled with tears. In 1597, William Waad (1546–1623), Lieutenant of the Tower of London, informed Sir Robert Cecil of a 'poor old man' who had been a recusant Catholic all his life and who, under examination, had confessed 'with tears' in his eyes – eyes which had now been opened 'to see the darkness that he had lived in'.

Sir Robert Cecil (1563–1612)

The son of William Cecil, who was Secretary of State for much of Elizabeth I's reign, Robert was one of the most important statesmen in the final years of the Tudor period and the early years of James VI and I, acting as Secretary of State during the succession. Just five foot four, he also suffered from a hunched back. Elizabeth called him 'my pygmy'.

Similarly, in a confession addressed to Elizabeth I in 1571, William Barker (fl.1540–76), secretary to the Duke of Norfolk, sought her forgiveness for his role in the failed Ridolfi plot – an attempt to assassinate her and replace her with Mary, Queen of Scots – humbly prostrating himself at her feet (albeit on paper) and describing himself figuratively as

> upon my Knees, with bitter Tears in myn Eyes, skarslie sufficient to finishe this Letter by Night, for lack of that Helpe that wastyd Eyes do want.

Barker was condemned to death, but the execution was never carried out.

While distrustful eyes marked the traitor, therefore, tear-filled ones were the sign of a penitent subject.

A LOVER'S EYES

Eyes could express loyalty to the monarch as well as penitence, and were used by Robert Dudley, Earl of Leicester and a long-term favourite of Elizabeth I, as a form of secret communication in one of his last letters to the queen. Writing from Tilbury on Saturday 3 August during the summer of the Spanish Armada, Leicester reassured his sovereign that her soldiers were as 'forwardly bent' as any in the world and that God himself 'fighteth for you, and your enymyes fall before you', signing his letter her 'most faythfull & most obedient ~~'. This symbol, representing a set of eyebrows, signalled the queen's nickname for her handsome favourite, which was 'Eyes'.

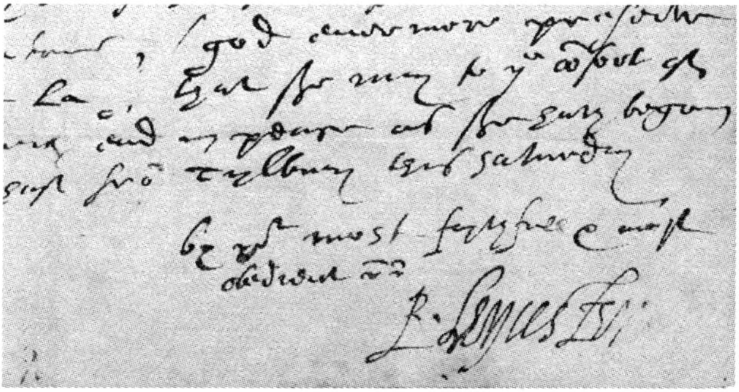

Elsewhere in the manuscript, Leicester drew eyebrows over the letter 'o' in the word 'moost'.

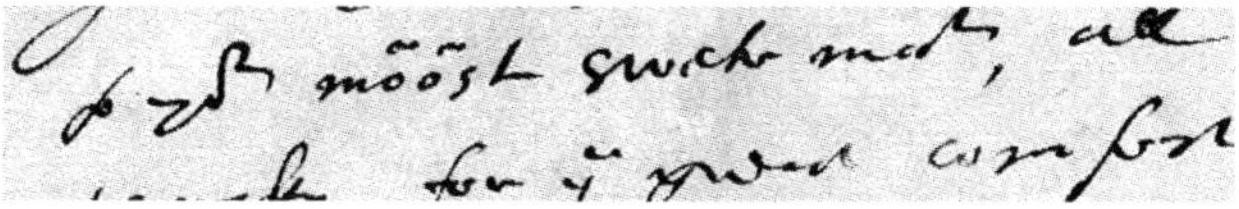

The nature of Elizabeth's relationship and feelings for Leicester – the dashing Robert Dudley of her youth – has long been a matter of some conjecture. But here, in the romantic symbolism of eyes in this coded correspondence, is a glimpse of the degree of intimacy between the two. On hearing the news of Leicester's death a month later, Elizabeth was said to be inconsolable, retiring to her private chamber where she 'mourned alone'. On her death in 1603, a bejewelled box found by her bedside was said to contain Leicester's last letter, testimony perhaps of the love she bore for the man she called 'Eyes'.

·13·

THE FACE

Will Somers, Henry VIII's fool, and Henry playing the harp, from Henry's Psalter, British Museum

We know what the Tudors looked like…

ROYAL FACES

A surprising variety of people exist in Tudor portraiture – though, as you might expect, a good number of paintings that survive are of the wealthy: monarchs, noblemen and noblewomen and their children. In particular, we have a very good idea of what all the Tudor monarchs looked like. Numerous contemporary portraits survive of Henry VII, Henry VIII, Edward VI, Mary I and Elizabeth I, painted by some of the finest portrait artists of the age, including Hans Holbein, Marcus Gheeraerts the Younger, Nicholas Hilliard and Isaac Oliver.

There are, however, some very significant absentees from the immediate Tudor family – not least of which is Anne Boleyn. A handful of images *might* be of Anne, but none of them are contemporary and none of them look the same. The best idea we have comes from a description given by Francesco Sanuto, a Venetian diplomat, and he was not entirely flattering. To his eyes she was 'not one of the handsomest women in the world; she is of middling stature, swarthy complexion, long neck, wide mouth, bosom not much raised... and eyes, which are black and beautiful', while a more hostile account of her appearance at her coronation deemed that 'a wart disfigured her very much'.

The coronation of Anne Boleyn

Henry and Anne were married in secret, but Anne's coronation in Westminster Abbey in May 1533 was lavish. The day before the ceremony, she was carried through the streets of London sitting in a litter on cloth of gold. On the day itself, over a thousand cannons were fired. But the day was not a public success; Anne was openly mocked.

A GALLERY OF FACES

From the 1560s onwards, portraits also survive of the faces of a remarkable cross section of Tudor society well below the ranks of royalty and the aristocracy. Unlike formal paintings of the monarchy, many of these depictions were for private consumption rather than public display. Some were large, to be hung on the wall, while others were tiny, embedded in lockets or private chests, boxes or drawers, for personal appreciation and remembrance.

These paintings are of civic leaders, merchants, lawyers, clergy, actors, writers, scholars, and artisans such as embroiderers and goldsmiths. One such portrait, particularly noteworthy for its charming, intimate window into the Tudor world and the sheer variety of information it tells us about Tudor life, depicts Joan Alleyn (c.1573–1623), the wife of the Elizabethan actor Edward Alleyn and step-daughter of the theatrical manager Philip Henslowe. In it, she is painted in a black dress with ruff and long sleeves, and a black felt brimmed hat; she is holding patterned brown and red gloves and a small red book. The portrait informs us about fashion: how women of the middling sort dressed, or at least how they wished to be represented, as well as the ubiquity of hats and gloves during this period. The small leather-bound book that she holds in her right hand gestures to female reading practices; it perhaps contains devotional literature, which would indicate her religious piety.

We even have a handful of images of the poor, marginalized, disabled and those with learning difficulties. Notable are those of Will Somers, Henry VIII's fool – whose comic visage appears in several contemporary portraits – as well as Jane the Fool, who joined Princess Mary's household and on occasion had her head shaved (a mark of the jester). Will is depicted in several paintings with a comic or rustic face, and in the *Family of Henry VIII* painting dating from circa 1545 he is depicted in the right-hand archway with a monkey on his shoulder, while Jane is painted in the left-hand archway looking a little lost and confused.

PREGNANCY PORTRAITS

One of the rarest of Tudor faces is that of the visibly pregnant woman, but a handful of portraits do exist. The paucity of them in the historical record is interesting, as many women spent a large proportion of their adult lives pregnant in a period where dynasty was of the utmost importance.

The examples that were produced are striking, and the period 1580 to 1630 saw the 'pregnancy portrait' emerge as a distinct subgenre of British painting. Such portraits were visual demonstrations of expected dynastic success. Perhaps the finest is that of Lady Katherine Knollys (née Carey) (c.1523–69), niece of Anne Boleyn, first cousin of Elizabeth I and one of the four Ladies of the Bedchamber. She is shown in a beautiful gown with a vertical chain (depicting the Greek god Mars) and a ribbon tied around her bump, accompanied by a small brown spaniel. In 1540, Katherine married the courtier Sir Francis Knollys (c.1512–96) and bore him twelve children. She was pregnant at least six times in eight years, between 1542 and 1550.

What is remarkable about Katherine's portrait is what we know about the actual painting of her face. Technical analysis on the portrait pioneered at the Yale Center for British Art, including infrared photography and microscopic examinations of paint layers, reveals a rather complex pictorial facial history. The artist – thought to be the Dutchman Steven van der Meulen – conceived the face in bold general terms, before adding minute details. There are also two sets of eyes, one half an inch below the other, which were painted over during composition; and in the nineteenth century the face was overpainted during a restoration. Conservation teams are working to restore the painting to its original state.

Pregnancy portrait of Katherine Carey, Lady Knollys

AGEING

Portraits, however, are not the only means of studying the Tudor appearance. One of the most intriguing questions raised by a variety of sources is how the Tudors aged, and how the ageing process was witnessed and understood. It is important, because the proportion of elderly people in the period was surprisingly high. Censuses of the poor taken in Norwich in 1570, Warwick in 1586 and Ipswich in 1635 recorded that some 26 per cent of the male population and 19 per cent of the female population admitted to being over sixty years of age.

Broadside ballads, one of the most popular forms of printed material in Tudor times – printed on a single side of inexpensive paper and widely available – are particularly valuable for understanding the ageing process. They record numerous signs of getting old, from loss of balance and eyesight to changes in the face. There are few surprises here, but the way in which the Tudors recorded and dealt with the ageing process is fascinating. One ballad lamented:

> The wrynklles in my browe,
> The furros in my facce,
> Say the lymping age must lodge hym now
> Wher you the must gyve hyme placce.

Another complained:

> When my Hairs grow hoary
> and my Cheeks look pale,
> When my Forehead has wrinkles
> and my Eye-Sight does fail

These signs of ageing (as well as marks left by the ravages of smallpox) could be overridden with a variety of Tudor cosmetics, including lead and mercury, which were used to paint and wash faces. As another ballad suggests:

> ... with Comb of black lead,
> With Paint white and Red,
> With Patch and wash,
> vamps up grey Ladies.

Less toxic and no doubt less corrosive was the method advised in John Partridge's household manual *The Treasurie of Commodious Conceits* (1573), which included a recipe to make 'a fayre face' that involved boiling flowers and leaves with white wine.

A HIDDEN TRUTH

Portrait painters could also use their skills to disguise reality, and so historians must learn not to be duped by certain Tudor faces. The ageing Elizabeth I, for example, was painted in glittering beauty in the formal portraits of her declining years, but they contrast powerfully with written descriptions of the queen from the same time.

In the 'Armada portrait' of 1588 she is painted with clear, firm skin and lustrous hair, and four years later she was painted positively aglow in the 'Ditchley portrait' (c.1592). However, the French ambassador reported in a dispatch of 1595:

> As for her face, it is and appears to be very aged. It is long and thin, and her teeth are very yellow and unequal, compared with what they were formerly, so they say, and on the left side less than on the right. Many of them are missing so that one cannot understand her easily when she speaks quickly.

Similarly, the German visitor Paul Hentzner described the queen in 1598 as majestic, yet 'her face [was] oblong, fair, but wrinkled; her eyes small, yet black and pleasant; her nose a little hooked; her lips narrow, and her teeth black... she wore false hair, and... her bosom was uncovered.'

Elizabeth I's Armada Portrait, 1588

The Armada portrait

One of the most famous portraits of Elizabeth I but created by an unknown artist. The queen is shown with numerous symbols of majesty, her hand resting possessively over a map of the Americas, while in the background the Armada is depicted in the midst of its defeat, blown onto rocks by a 'Protestant Wind'.

·14·

BELLS

Hampton Court clock and bell tower

Bells were all about Tudor state propaganda…

EVERYDAY BELL-RINGING

Bell-ringing (or campanology) was an important part of the soundscape of Tudor England. Bells were rung on a variety of occasions for a variety of reasons. It was a powerful and effective way to send a message: a church bell could be heard as much as a mile away, and in the mid-Tudor period an estimated 10,000 churches with bells could be found across the length and breadth of the country. The Bishop of Worcester, and later chaplain to Edward VI, Hugh Latimer (c.1487–1555) said that, 'if all the bells in England should be rung together at a certain hour, I think there would be almost no place but some bells might be heard there'.

Some bell-ringing occasions were straightforward: they were rung with regularity to summon people to prayer; with joy at weddings; with solemnity at funerals; in celebration on feast days; with urgency as alarms to summon people into the street. But because bell-ringing was such an effective tool for those wishing to communicate thoughts or beliefs nationwide, it was also harnessed for political or religious ends throughout the Tudor period.

THE ATTACK ON BELLS

During the English Reformation, the state launched an attack on church bells; by controlling how and when bells were rung and for what purpose, they controlled religious practice and beliefs. Throughout the medieval period, church bells had been an important part of the fabric of Christian worship: they were rung for religious services; for marking time; to indicate the status of religious leaders; for the dead and the dying; to celebrate mass with the elevation of the host; and to invoke Mary and the saints.

However, the Swiss Reformer Heinrich Bullinger (1504–75), whose ideas were influential in mid-Tudor England, saw bell-ringing as deeply superstitious, as it was so clearly connected with traditional Catholic worship and ritual. The biblical translator William Tyndale also challenged the sacred status of 'hallowed bells'. He wrote:

> Thou wilt say do not such things bring the holy ghost and put away sin and drive away sprites [when in fact they] bring us from the true faith that is in God's word unto a superstitious and a false belief of our own imaginacion.

By the reign of the young Protestant king Edward VI, the ringing of the sacring bell, one of the most important bells in Catholic worship, was prohibited. This particular bell had

William Tyndale (c.1494–1536)

A scholar well known for translating the Bible into English, his version was the first to make use of the printing press and helped spread the ideas of the Reformation around the world. Captured in Antwerp in 1535 by agents of Charles V, he was found guilty of heresy, strangled and then burned at the stake.

traditionally been rung to announce the moment of transubstantiation – the conversion of bread and wine into the body and blood of Christ – during the celebration of the Eucharist, but it was silenced in 1547 when the Church of England sought to purge itself of this doctrine.

The Reformation period did not see an outright elimination of church bells, however. Instead, Catholic bell-ringing was replaced by reformed Protestant practices. The sacring bell, for example, was replaced by the sermon bell, which was rung to signify the start of the sermon.

NATIONAL CELEBRATIONS

While bell-ringing was reformed in religious services during the mid-sixteenth century, it was also adopted for secular political ends. Bells were rung on occasions linked with significant national events, and here their language became more complex.

It is possible to reconstruct major events on which bells were rung by studying churchwardens' accounts, which not only recorded when the bells were rung but also the associated expenditure to pay the ringers or provide them with food and drink. We know, for example, that in 1570 the West Country parish of Ashburton paid four pence for 'ale for the ringing at the rejoicing for the coronation and divine continuation of the reign of the Queen'.

From sources like this we can see that bells were rung on the coronations or deaths of each of the Tudor monarchs; but the practice of bell-ringing becomes more interesting still when you consider questions such as how long the bells were rung for and how loudly. In some respects, bell-ringing was like a barometer that reflected local anxieties and the national mood. Long and loud ringing was a keen sign of political support.

In the West Country, the bells were rung long and loud after Henry VIII's death, but less so for his son Edward VI; they were rung loudly at the accession of Mary, but more loudly still at the accession of Elizabeth – and then regularly, loudly and for a long time on each anniversary of Elizabeth's accession, in a formal celebration of her Protestant rule that became known as 'crownation day'.

LOYALTY

During both Mary's and Elizabeth's reigns, bell-ringing was a widespread way of demonstrating allegiance to the incumbent regime. Bells were sounded on news of Mary's pregnancy, and then, prematurely and incorrectly, in the belief that she would bear a son.

Under Elizabeth, this practice became even more commonplace. Bells were rung when Thomas Percy, the Earl of Northumberland, was captured in 1570 after the failure of the Rising of the North, an attempt to depose Elizabeth I; they were rung in 1585 and 1586 when the Parry and Babington plots to assassinate Elizabeth were uncovered; when the Catholic Mary, Queen of Scots, who had a dynastic claim to Elizabeth's throne, was beheaded in 1587; when the Royal Navy defeated the Spanish Armada in 1588 and England was saved from Spanish, Catholic invasion; and when the Royal Navy captured the crucial port of Cádiz from Spain in 1596, a reprisal for the Armada.

The Rising of the North of 1569

Another Catholic plot designed to replace Elizabeth I with Mary, Queen of Scots, conceived by northern English noblemen. The rebel army, which had occupied Durham and captured nearby Barnard Castle, dispersed into Scotland when confronted by forces raised by the Earl of Sussex.

Of even more significance is that fact that such bell-ringing was both approved and encouraged by Elizabeth's Privy Council, and you could get into trouble if you did not toe the line. In 1563, for example, Elizabeth was serenaded by church bells as she travelled by water through London, from Whitehall to Greenwich, but those churches who failed to participate in this 'spontaneous' act of joy at the sight of the monarch were fined six shillings and eight pence – making what was, at the time, a significant hole in church coffers. Although it remains unclear if the Privy Council actually initiated the idea, it is certain that, under Elizabeth, some bell-ringing was nothing short of state propaganda.

ANNOYANCE AND DANGER

The general population's attitudes towards bells were mixed. For some, the pealing of bells was cause for joy: 'it is natural to the mind of man to be ravished with great joy by the notes and harmony of music' wrote one Elizabethan minister; while in 1582 the Mayor of Bedford had finally had enough and complained of 'the intolerable trouble to others' caused by the vicar's bell-ringing.

This type of annoyance could carry religious overtones. A 1566 letter from Antwerp to the merchant and financier Sir Thomas Gresham described how the 'Papists' had been 'ringing the bells all day', which meant that the city's Protestants had been 'unable to hear their preachers'. And in 1551, John Hooper, Bishop of Gloucester, demanded the suppression of bells in order to prevent 'oppressing of the sound of the minister that readeth the word of God'.

For one unfortunate individual, John Robinson of Cobham in Kent, bell-ringing was not merely an annoyance but a dangerous and fatal activity. At some point between eight and nine at night, in an unidentified month in 1592, the hapless John stood on a bench to reach the bell-rope because it was too short for him. But when he pulled it down, the rope wrapped around the end of the bench and pulled him six feet into the air, from where he fell onto his head, dying the next day.

·15·

SHRINKING

The Drake Jewel, c.1586

By thinking small the Tudors were able to achieve great things…

MINIATURE PORTRAITS

The Tudors considered miniature portraits to be the very apogee of artistic skill. These tiny paintings first began to appear in illuminated manuscripts in the fifteenth century, but became an artistic form in their own right when specialist artists reached an unprecedented level of skill during the Tudor period.

One of the most important miniatures to have survived the centuries is known as the 'Drake Jewel', an exquisite jewel of gold, enamel and rubies finished with a huge pearl hanging from its base like a pendulum. On one side is a locket with a tiny portrait of Queen Elizabeth by Nicholas Hilliard (1547–1619), the finest miniaturist of the age; the inside of the lid contains parchment painted with a phoenix, an image commonly associated with the queen.

The jewel was presented personally by Elizabeth in 1588 to the sailor and adventurer Sir Francis Drake (c.1540–96), the first Englishman to sail around the world and only the second man in history to do so.

Miniature portraits were commonly given as intimate gifts by the queen to those she wished to reward, testimony of her regal authority but also a sign of royal favour. On another occasion Drake was presented with a second miniature of Elizabeth, which depicted her in a sunburst and was intended to be worn in his hat. The Drake Jewel itself was indicative of the close relationship forged between Elizabeth and Drake, a man who had risen from being the son of a farmer and preacher to the Queen's champion.

A BOOK OF ASTROLOGY

These miniatures do not just survive as individual portraits. One of the most wonderful collections of miniatures can be found in a book on astrology, compiled for Henry VII in the 1490s and illustrated by a Flemish master illustrator working alongside English artists. The manuscript, now held in the collections of the British Library, contains no fewer than forty-three unique miniatures.

Such miniatures are an exceptional historical source that shine a bright light on numerous aspects of Tudor life. The miniatures in Henry VII's astrology book, for example, have helped us to appreciate the Tudor understanding of the celestial world as well as the international diplomatic relations between England, France and Spain in the late fifteenth century, various aspects of monarchy and even fashion.

The finest miniature in the manuscript, one which encapsulates all of these themes, depicts an English king, enthroned under a canopy bearing the royal arms of France and England, being presented with a book. He is wearing a newly fashionable imperial crown and carries a sceptre. He is splendidly dressed in robes of gold silk decorated with roses and his mantle is decorated with pomegranates – the emblem of Catherine of Aragon. The man presenting the book, who can be identified from the arms beautifully illustrated on his shield as Louis II, Duke of Orléans, is wearing a magnificent blue coat trimmed with fur. Such sources bring Tudor history alive in the most vivid way possible.

Catherine of Aragon (1485–1536)

The Spanish first wife of Henry VIII and widow of his brother, Prince Arthur. Mother of Mary I, she was unable to produce a male heir and was divorced by Henry, who then married Anne Boleyn.

SHIP PLANS

Something else that the Tudors became very good at shrinking was the ship. It was in this period that shipwrights, using pioneering mathematical techniques, first began to understand how to turn an enormous, three-dimensional wooden warship into a two-dimensional scale drawing, immortalizing it on a piece of paper. This was the period when the paper 'ship plan' was invented.

It was an enormous breakthrough and meant two important things: firstly, that other shipwrights could study a particular ship design; and secondly, that ship designs could be replicated. This made it easier to learn from past mistakes, as techniques could be studied, debated and adapted. It also meant that ships could be made of a similar 'class'. Fleets therefore became more homogenized, which made them easier to manage, repair and operate. The invention of the paper ship plan was one of the most significant breakthroughs in the entire history of seafaring, and a cornerstone in the construction of British maritime power.

The man primarily responsible for this change was a brilliant mathematician, shipwright and innovator called Mathew Baker, who personally oversaw the construction and repair of many of the ships that fought the Spanish Armada in 1588. Fortunately for us, Baker also wrote a manuscript later entitled *Fragments of*

Ancient English Shipwrightry, which survives today in the Pepys Library at Magdalene College, Cambridge, and has single-handedly transformed our understanding of this breakthrough.

Mathew Baker (c.1530–1613)

The son of Henry VIII's shipwright James Baker, shipbuilding was in Mathew Baker's blood. In 1572 he was appointed Master Shipwright in the royal dockyards, and in 1576 he built the *Gabriel*, the flagship of the privateer and explorer Martin Frobisher. But he constantly feuded with other shipbuilders and the naval commander John Hawkins criticized his idleness, writing that 'he hath laboured with the rest of that idle company to return to their old vomit'.

One of the most important images in the manuscript shows Baker working at a desk – not at a shipyard – poring over a ship design with ruler and dividers, allowing him to

Shipwrights drawing, *Fragments of Ancient Shipwrightry* by Matthew Baker (1586)

work to scale. We also know that Baker personally oversaw apprentices learning the new art – including Phineas Pett (1570–1647), who later became Master Shipwright to both James I and Charles I.

SPIES

The Tudor obsession with shrinking also extended to the underground world of the spy. A fundamental weapon in the dark arts of cryptography and espionage was the ability to communicate in a manner that went undetected, below the radar of the Tudor state. Making things small and easily hidden was central to the smuggling of secret letters, which were folded into tiny packets that could be secreted on the person or hidden in items such as staffs, pots and even eggs.

One of the most ingenious and unexpected methods for clandestine correspondence was to write a message sufficiently small that it could be folded up and hidden on one's person by being innocuously stitched into clothing. The seventeen-year-old recusant Thomas Cauze of Drayton was apprehended in 1595 in Chester, on his way to Spain, with a letter in Latin sewed up in his doublet; and in 1591, one Reynold Bisley carried letters into England sewn 'in his [coat] Buttons'. A similar technique was used by the Elizabethan Jesuit priest John Gerard, who sent letters of recommendation for two boys travelling to St Omer, the paper being 'wrapped around one or two collars to make it look as if it was being used to keep the collars clean'; interestingly, the letters were also written in lemon-juice invisible ink.

·16·

ACCIDENTS

Engraving of an accident near water from Everard Digby's *De arte natandi* (1587)

Life in Tudor Britain was riddled with danger…

EVERYDAY ACCIDENTS

We know an unexpectedly large amount about Tudor accidents because of the survival of coroners' reports. The reports, which number in the thousands, offer a unique perspective on everyday Tudor life. Written almost entirely in Latin, these fascinating vellum rolls detail fatal hazards and accidental deaths of people from all walks of Tudor society – young and old, male and female, rich and poor, healthy and infirm – because coroners were charged to investigate and report on all violent or unnatural deaths. They tell us how, throughout the year, people drowned in cesspits, were mauled by bears, crushed by carts, mangled by windmills, trampled by horses, cut by scythes and shot by firearms. One man, Henry Pert of Welbeck, Nottinghamshire, even managed to achieve the almost physically impossible feat of shooting himself in the head with his longbow.

Christmas appears to have been one of the most dangerous times of year, a combination of cold weather, festive feasting and drunkenness. On Christmas Day 1533, the Oxfordshire spinster Jane Grene of Eynsham climbed the stairs to her room at nine o'clock in the evening, but, a little worse for wear from yuletide revelry, she missed her footing, tumbled backwards down the stairs, hit her head on a stone in the wall, which broke her skull 'through to the brain', and broke her neck. And on Boxing Day 1563, John Hypper, while playing 'Christenmas games with divers other parishioners of Houghton, Hampshire', 'involuntarily' crushed himself and injured his testicles so badly that, two days later, he died.

MIRACLE CURES

Other sources are surprisingly informative about accidents, too, and reveal just how widespread they were. One of the most remarkable is a print from a woodcut engraving which dates from the reign of Henry VII and was discovered pasted into the rear flyleaf of a copy of the Bible held in the archives of the Bodleian Library in Oxford.

The print shows Henry's uncle, Henry VI, at the centre of a shambled group of eight people, four of whom have been severely injured. These people have come to the king for a miracle cure, and it is likely that they were based on real people and real events, and that their stories actually survive in a separate book recording the 'miracles' worked by the king.

The woman in the group who is shown with a knife in her throat, for example, is thought to be the nine-year-old Joan Barton, who is known to have accidentally fallen onto a knife, stabbing herself in the throat; the man with the arrow in his chest could well be Reginald Scarborough, who is recorded to have suffered such an injury during archery practice in the village of South Luffenham, Rutland; and there is even an image of a wax effigy of a man with a hole in his torso, which is likely to relate to the appalling story of Henry Walter de Guildford, whose body was pierced by a cannonball without it actually killing him. All of these people were believed to have come to the king and to have benefited from his miraculous powers of healing.

TUDOR HEALTH AND SAFETY

Such ever-present and unexpected dangers posed a significant problem in the workplace, which was where nearly half of all fatal accidents in Tudor Britain happened. But Tudor society was not unaware of health and safety issues, and a series of popular pamphlets advised on safety.

A copy of one of these, Thomas Tusser's *Five Hundred Points of Good Husbandry* (1573), could be found in almost every one of the 8,600 parishes of England. The instructional poem included advice on subjects as varied as how to keep carts 'wel clowted and greased' before hay time began, how farmhands should work their fields diagonally to avoid being severed by another labourer's scythe, and how to climb trees safely to kill crows. 'Beware how ye climber', he warned, 'for breaking your neck.'

CHILDHOOD MISHAPS

It is frustratingly difficult for historians to reconstruct the history of childhood from a young person's perspective, as so few first-hand accounts written by children survive. Reports of accidents involving Tudor children, however, shed a light on this secret world. One sad tale relayed in a 1569 coroner's report describes the tragic death of the two-and-a-half-year-old Jane Shaxspere, who drowned while picking marigolds in Upton Warren, close to William Shakespeare's birthplace, Stratford-upon-Avon. It is, perhaps, not too far-fetched to imagine her as a possible source for Ophelia in Shakespeare's *Hamlet* (1599–1602).

Ophelia

A young Danish noblewoman, she is driven mad by the fact that her lover, Prince Hamlet, kills her father, Polonius. She climbs into a willow tree over a river but the branch breaks and she drowns. Shakespeare does not make it clear if it is suicide or an accident. *Hamlet* was one of Shakespeare's most popular plays during his lifetime.

As a supplement to coroners' records, the diary of John Dee, the Elizabethan mathematician and astrologer, records the countless accidents that befell his own children and sheds an important light on the rough and tumble of childish games.

The younger members of the Dee family appear to have been unusually accident-prone. On 3 July 1582, John's son Arthur fell from the top of the stairs and 'cut his forehead on the right eyebrow', and the same boy was later 'wounded on his head by his own wanton throwing of a brick-bat' which weighed twenty-one pounds, the weight of three house-bricks. On New Year's Day 1588, another son, Michael – 'going childishly with a sharp stick of eight inches long' – fell in his sister's room, the sharp point piercing his left eye next to his nose with a 'great abundance of blood'. The boy was lucky not to have been blinded, for which Dee praised God 'for his mercies and protection'. Arthur was injured again when he had his nose 'wantonly' cut by a razor; and Dee's daughter Katherine was hit so hard on the ear by her mother that her nose bled profusely for more than an hour, the severity of the blow having apparently burst an artery.

·17·

FRUIT-EATING

Portrait of Queen Elizabeth I by Steven van der Meulen, c.1563

Fruit-eating was a defining characteristic of Tudor life…

PUTREFYING FEVERS

For much of the Tudor period, eating fruit was considered bad for you; at best, commentators were lukewarm in recommending its consumption. We know this because numerous pamphlets were written throughout the sixteenth century that offered forms of dietary advice. 'Doctors of Physcke' understood the working of the human body in terms of the balance of its four 'humours' – black bile, yellow bile, blood and phlegm. Fruit, particularly if eaten fresh rather than cooked, was believed to upset this carefully tuned system because it was both cold and wet, which would, it was thought, only worsen the body's response to the cold and wet English climate, turning one's blood into phlegm.

In his popular health book *The Castel of Helth* (1541), Sir Thomas Elyot wrote that, although fruit had once been an important part of man's diet, bodies had changed and it was now harmful, leading to 'ill humors' and 'putrified fevers'. Apples, he told his readers, were 'colde, hard to digest' and made 'corrupted bloudde'; the medlar fruit (which Shakespeare termed 'open-arse' for its bottomly appearance, following the French cul-de-chien), he advised constricted and strained the stomach and induced 'melancholye'. Another contemporary writer, Dr Walter Baley, in his *A Briefe Treatise Touching the Preservation of the Eie Sight* (1602), specifically outlined the danger that eating raw fruit could have on the eyes – which physicians believed depended upon heat and dryness for their health.

Sir Thomas Elyot (c.1490–1546)

A leading diplomat under Henry VIII who travelled to the court of the Holy Roman Emperor Charles V to persuade him to support Henry's divorce of Catherine of Aragon. Elyot was also a scholar, and wrote the earliest comprehensive Latin-English dictionary. His book *The Castel of Helth* was designed to make ancient medical knowledge accessible to those who did not read Greek.

This did not mean, however, that all fruit was considered bad all of the time. Tudor medicinal beliefs were nothing if not complex and often contradictory: for many, fruit was deemed to have important health-related properties. Household manuals of the period commonly feature medical recipes that incorporate fruit as one of their ingredients. Writing on the matter of plums in his *Dyets Dry Dinner* (1599), the Cambridge scholar Henry Butts felt that, although they corrupted the humours of cold and weak people and were hurtful to the aged, the fact that they loosened the stomach made them beneficial for treating constipation.

THE FASHIONABILITY OF FRUIT

Despite the warnings of dietary writers, fruit was widely consumed throughout the sixteenth century. There was an abundance of wild fruit trees in the hedgerows, which made seasonal foraging for wild cherries, plums, damsons, apples, pears, quince, medlars, strawberries, whortleberries (bilberries) and sloes a popular activity among neighbouring poor – providing them with an invaluable and vitamin-rich supplement to their diet. In addition, monasteries and great houses cultivated their own orchards, which supplied the kitchens of these establishments. When Henry VIII built Nonsuch Palace, he incorporated the fruit trees of nearby Syon Abbey – now available to the king after the Dissolution of the Monasteries.

The widespread eating of the domestic fruit crop was augmented by a growth in both the variety and quantity of imported exotic fruits, revealing trading networks that spread halfway around the world. Grapes, in the form of raisins and currants, were common imports during the sixteenth century, as were figs, oranges, peaches, olives, dates and medlars. A huge variety of foreign varieties were also home-grown, producing a fabulous cornucopia. In the early 1600s, for example, we know that no fewer than sixty-four varieties of pears were available in England. Imports of particularly high value were 'blue' figs, shipped from the Far East. The evidence for this supply of exotic figs comes from a range of written accounts and recipes but also from archaeology, as seeds can be excavated, dated and identified.

A growing scientific curiosity in botany and an increasing fashionability of gardens among social elites, together with the new discoveries of seafarers and increased contact with foreign food cultures, meant that the growing and eating of fruit rose in popularity in the Tudor period – it ceased to be the despised food of the poor and became a trendy food of the rich. In 1561, for example, the fruit purchased by the Earl of Derby (combined with luxurious spices) totalled a whopping 131 pounds, 3 shillings and 4 pence, or 8.1 per cent of his annual expenditure on food and drink in that year. A fascinating array of fruity treats were also prepared by the servants of Robert

Dudley, Earl of Leicester, for the visit of Queen Elizabeth to Kenilworth Castle in 1575. Dudley's household accounts list the purchase of highly prized foreign delicacies including peaches, pomegranates and Jordanian almonds, as well as quinces, strawberries and citrus fruits. The earl himself was very fond of such treats and even had a special comfit box, ornately decorated with gold and silver ribbon, in which he kept sweetmeats. A fascinating relic of Tudor fruit-eating, it survives in the collections of the Victoria and Albert Museum in London.

Robert Dudley (1532–88)

One of the greatest landowners of the Tudor period, Dudley was involved in both domestic and foreign politics. Few other men were as influential in the Elizabethan court - he was a favourite of Elizabeth I and her regular dancing partner. Dudley was in overall command of the English land forces during the Spanish Armada threat but died from natural causes shortly afterwards.

We also know from court correspondence that, on her visit to Kenilworth, Elizabeth enjoyed walking in the magnificent gardens there and helped herself to strawberries, cherries and 'other frutes' straight from the vine, stalk or branch. Contrary to physicians' advice, it seems the queen couldn't resist the taste of a fresh strawberry, something she had in common with labourers of the period.

FRUIT-EATING ABOARD SHIP

On Tudor ships, the subject of fruit-eating is markedly different from what we see on land: there was very little of it. As a young man, the English admiral Nathaniel Butler (born c.1577) had served in Elizabeth's navy as a common sailor. Later in life he noted how English sailors were 'besotted' with their uniquely fruit-free maritime diet, born of the need to preserve food for the uncertain duration of a voyage.

We know from the archaeological evidence of the *Mary Rose*, in which 100 plum stones were beautifully preserved, that some fruit was consumed at sea, especially on operations near to shore, but the mainstay of a sailor's diet was hard biscuit occasionally augmented with meat, fish stock, butter and cheese. This all lacked vitamin C, a deficiency that could cause serious illness in the long term, but Butler believed the English sailors would rather suffer scurvy 'than to be weaned from their customary diet, or to lose the least bit of it'. He also noted how this diet was markedly different from that of French, Spanish and Dutch sailors, who enjoyed fruit when they could, particularly olives and figs. Interestingly, the diet of Tudor soldiers also seems to have been devoid of fruit, no doubt a reflection of the extra care that had to be taken when transporting fresh fruit to prevent it from spoiling: the army had no time for such delicacies.

·18·

LETTER-WRITING

Portrait of Penelope Lady Rich by Nicholas Hilliard

Letter-writing was all about female power and persuasion…

POLITICAL INFLUENCE

One of the most accomplished female letter-writers of the Tudor period was Lady Penelope Rich (1563–1607), whose mastery of the art allowed her to assume a role of significant political influence. The daughter of Walter Devereux, Earl of Essex, Lady Rich was well-connected and highly educated. She was a skilled linguist, having been instructed at home in French, Spanish and Italian, and had received lessons in history, philosophy, rhetoric, arithmetic and the literary arts. Her surviving letters reveal a mastery of the complexities of Tudor letter-writing.

Penelope Rich enjoyed wide-ranging contact with writers across Europe and even conducted secret correspondence, employing ciphers and codes. She utilized her letters for patronage and diplomatic ends, acting as a political intermediary – operating through the influence of her brother Robert, 2nd Earl of Essex, and powerful court connections. The Warwickshire gentleman Sir Humphrey Ferrers even considered her to have sufficient power to ask her to petition the queen on his behalf for a barony.

Lady Rich's considerable skills are best demonstrated by her intimate involvement in her brother's overtures to the Scottish king, James VI, Elizabeth's eventual successor. Essex wanted to ingratiate himself with James and his sister was a useful intermediary, and so she wrote in secret to the Scottish monarch. The weekly letters were written in secret code and much appreciated by the king, who 'commended much the fineness of her wit, the invention and well writing'. Although the escapade eventually failed, it illustrates the important ways in which women letter-writers were able to intercede in politics at the very highest level.

LETTERS FROM THE PALACE

There was no higher level than the English monarch's court, and letters surviving in the archive of the indomitable Elizabethan matriarch and ambitious dynast Bess of Hardwick (c.1527–1608), Countess of Shrewsbury, reveal a detailed news and intelligence network that extended internationally.

The countess was regularly supplied with private and personalized news from her female contacts at Elizabeth's court. Their letters largely concerned the status of her general standing and favour with the queen, the monarch's reactions to her gifts, and the progress of suits. In one letter, Lady Wingfield, 'Mother of the Maids [of honour]' at court, wrote that the queen in conversation had stated, 'I assure you there is no lady in this land that I better love.' Royal favour and intimacy of this sort had important symbolic resonance, since reputation had practical implications, and letter-writing activities for Tudor women allowed them to cultivate social and court contacts and stay connected with current affairs.

Letters were important instruments of power, and Bess of Hardwick's correspondence network allowed her to achieve significant influence. When absent from London, she received letters from family, servants, friends, wider social contacts and semi-professional newsletter-writers, keeping her current

Maids of Honour

Young unmarried girls who attended on the queen in the royal household, distinct from the senior court positions of ladies-in-waiting and gentlewomen of the bedchamber. During the Tudor period aristocratic families put great effort into securing positions as maids of honour for their daughters, as a way of advancing their own political interests, building their patronage networks, and in the hope of transacting a good marriage. Many of the most well-known Tudor women, such as Lady Jane Grey, once served as maids of honour. As a group the maids were looked after by a senior female courtier, who was known as the Mother-of-the-Maids.

with court and national events as well as news from the capital. When at court or absent from one of her residences, she received regular reports from her servants, estate stewards and legal advisers on various matters: household and estate management, children and other family members, the numerous legal cases in which she was involved, the progress of her building works, and local events. Her son-in-law (and stepson) Gilbert Talbot sent her 'suche newes as on the Quenes hye wayes we have mett'. The countess was also regularly kept up to date on the latest religious and political developments in Europe by correspondents who recycled for her the contents of continental newsletters, which was extremely useful at a time when she and her (later-to-be-estranged) husband were keepers of Mary, Queen of Scots during her imprisonment in England.

PLEAS FOR ASSISTANCE

For women involved in both family and business disputes, letter-writing allowed them an opportunity to represent and defend themselves, to assert their rights and to mobilize powerful allies through persuasive words.

The business letters of Elizabeth Howard (c.1497–1558), Duchess of Norfolk, are an important example. In letters to Thomas Cromwell, Henry VIII's chief minister, she begged him to intervene in her disastrous marriage and catalogued the violence she had received at the hands of her estranged husband, Thomas Howard, Duke of Norfolk, and his mistress, Elizabeth Holland. In one letter, she denounced the 'bawd' and 'harlots' that her husband kept in his house, describing how 'they bound me and pinnacled me, and sat on my breast till I spit blood, which I have been worse for ever since'.

Thomas Howard, third duke of Norfolk (1473–1554)

A prominent Tudor nobleman, courtier and politician, who was the head of the famous Howard dynasty, and one of the richest men during the reign of Henry VIII. He was the uncle of Anne Boleyn and Catherine Howard, both of whom lost the heads when they fell out of favour with their royal husband, and Norfolk was active in scheming for the matches. He fell from favour in 1546 and was imprisoned in the Tower, at a time when his son Henry Howard, earl of Surrey was executed for treason. On the accession of Mary I his political favour was rehabilitated having helped the Tudor queen secure her claim to the throne.

Letter-writing was possibly the only avenue that Elizabeth had for securing redress: she was ostracized by her family, who sought reconciliation between her and the duke and blamed what they saw as the duchess's violent conduct and language for the rift between the couple. By writing these letters to Cromwell, Elizabeth was attempting to secure help and make her appalling situation more widely known. 'I pray you shew my Lord my husband [this letter]', she wrote to Cromwell. Unfortunately, in this particular instance, her pleas went unanswered. As her husband was one of the most powerful noblemen in the realm, the state failed to intervene.

The importance of Elizabeth's entreaties lies not in the accuracies or inaccuracies of the reports of violence committed against her, but in the rhetorical forcefulness with which she described the brutal acts. Above all, letters of this sort were an exercise in the art of persuasive argument, demonstrating how Tudor women seized the pen as a weapon with which to defend themselves.

·19·

CANNIBALISM

Os Filhos de Pindorama. Cannibalism in Brazil in 1557

Cannibalism is all about civilization …

CANNIBALS IN LITERATURE

Cannibalism was a major theme in Tudor theatre, and Shakespeare is full of it. 'O God, that I were a man! I would eat his heart in the market-place', exclaims the character Beatrice in *Much Ado about Nothing* (1598–9). Meanwhile, the tragic Moorish general Othello (1603) 'bewitches' his wife Desdemona with tales of cannibals; the Roman general Coriolanus (1605–8) worries that the masses want to eat him; and most famously of all, in *The Merchant of Venice* (1596–9), the Jewish moneylender Shylock's desire for Antonio's 'pound of flesh' when he defaults on a loan is ridiculed as an unholy appetite.

Shakespeare and others knew very well that cannibalism worked effectively as a way of engaging a Tudor audience with contrasting themes of civilization and savagery. Cannibalism as the savage end of the extremes to which people might go was presented as a limit that should never be crossed.

The theme was perhaps explored most fully in the essay 'Of the Caniballes' (1580) by Michel de Montaigne (1533–92), one of the most significant philosophers of the period. It appeared in the 1603 translation of Montaigne's *Essays* and undoubtedly influenced Shakespeare's *The Tempest* (1610–11), which features themes, names and characters that have been traced to Montaigne.

Addressing the willingness of those in the sixteenth century to reduce tribal peoples of the New World to cannibalistic barbarians, Montaigne's complex argument uses this as a mirror to reflect on the 'savagery' of the Europeans themselves. In the essay, he focuses on the behaviour of the Tupinambá people of north-eastern Brazil, and describes how they roast and eat their prisoners 'and send some chops to their absent friends':

> I am not sorry that we should here take notice of the barbarous horror of so cruel an action, but that, seeing so clearly into their faults, we should be so blind to our own. I conceive there is more barbarity in eating a man alive, than when he is dead; in tearing a body limb from limb by racks and torments, that is yet in perfect sense; in roasting it by degrees; in causing it to be bitten and worried by dogs and swine...

Montaigne's essay was itself inspired by several other contemporary tracts on cannibalism, including *True History: An Account of Cannibal Captivity in Brazil* (1557) in which a German soldier, Hans Staden, describes his two trips to the New World.

Largely because of its depictions of cannibalism by the Tupinambá, Staden's *True History* became one of the best-selling travel narratives of the entire sixteenth century. It is not difficult to see why: it is written in numerous bite-sized chapters that all have excellent titles, such as 'How one of the Frenchmen who had been left by the ships among the savages came thither to see me, and advised them to eat me, as I was a Portuguese' and 'How they ate a prisoner and led me thereto'. In the latter chapter, he generously advises the terrified prisoner 'to be of good cheer, for they would only eat his flesh, but his soul would proceed to another place'.

FATTENING UP

The historical evidence for cannibalism in the New World is varied and fascinating. From the moment of earliest contact with the peoples they met there, the Spanish made a simple distinction: those who were cannibals and those who were not. Many of these early travel narratives were printed for an English market, including Sebastian Münster's *A Treatise of the Newe India* (1553), which described encountering natives who were 'accustomed to eate mannes fleshe'. Apparently, those the cannibals captured who were under the age of fourteen were castrated and then fattened up, in the manner of a good capon (a castrated domestic cockerel fattened for eating), while those over twenty were killed immediately, their guts pulled out, their flesh eaten fresh and their 'extreme partes' preserved in salt or pickled for later consumption.

But while the exotic nature of these detailed and lengthy narratives explains their subsequent popularity, the motivation behind the vivid descriptions was based on a law that cannibals could be enslaved. Spanish sources identifying cannibals, therefore, are not wholly reliable, as it was in the Spaniards' economic interests to identify as many cannibals as possible so these natives could be put to work on the new plantations.

One of the earliest English descriptions of cannibalism was written by Walter Ralegh, who travelled to the New World in 1594, though his accounts are not necessarily to be trusted because they also describe people 'whose heads are in their chests' and whose 'feet point backwards'. His most detailed description of cannibalism is of a people called the Arwacas, who lived south of the Orinoco. These people, he wrote, 'beat the bones of their lords into powder', which was then mixed into drinks. A tantalizing glimpse of alien life, it was enough to ignite an interest in cannibals that blossomed in the Tudor world.

Sir Walter Ralegh (c.1552–1618)

Tudor explorer, soldier and courtier, instrumental in the colonization of the Americas. In 1585, Raleigh was responsible for dispatching the expedition which founded the Roanoke Colony in North Carolina, the first English settlement in the New World. His experiences in South America helped create the myth of 'El Dorado', the city of gold. Always falling in and out of favour, Raleigh spent a good part of his adult life imprisoned in the Tower of London.

HYPOCRISY

A curious aspect about how the horrors of cannibalism enthralled Tudor audiences was that it was also a common aspect of Tudor medicine. While the cannibals of the New World were reviled for their savagery, the Tudors routinely – and hypocritically – ingested human blood, bones and fat as part of everyday cures for anything from epilepsy to headaches. Elizabeth I's surgeon John Banister (1532/3–c.1599) even recommended 'corpse medicine', which was made from body parts.

A key ingredient used at the time was Egyptian mummies. The geographer Richard Hakluyt (c.1552–1616) described in his monumental *The Principal Navigations, Voyages, Traffiques and*

Discoveries of the English Nation, Made by Sea or Over-land, to the Remote and Farthest Distant Quarters of the Earth... (1589) how, in Cairo, 'the bodies of ancient men, not rotten but all whole' were unearthed daily from a pyramid, with one of his fellow travellers adding 'these dead bodies are the Mummie which the Phisitians [Physicians] and Apothecaries doe against our willes make us to swallow'.

It is clear that such body parts found their way to England, with the writer and poet Thomas Nashe (1567–c.1601) remarking in 1594 that while for the general public 'Mummy is somewhat obscure', it was very 'familiar' to physicians. In 1586, the English succeeded in securing an illicit cargo of mummy-meat weighing over 600 pounds.

·20·

RINGS

Portrait of Princess Elizabeth, attributed to William Scrots, c.1546–7, close-up on rings

Tudor rings are all about emotion…

ETERNAL LOVE

Rings were one of the most precious personal belongings during the sixteenth century, and are central to understanding the emotional world of Tudor England. Rings could be used to pledge love, memorialize friendships and honour the dead.

One of the most commonly worn rings was the wedding ring, which functioned as a symbol of eternal love and devotion, a meaning that was manifested in the infinite circularity of the ring itself. There were several different styles of wedding ring: a gimmel ring (hoops), fede ring (clasped hands) and a poesie ring (which contained personalized verse). Rings engraved with short rhymes were popular from the medieval period onwards, and many examples survive. According to the English writer George Puttenham in his *Arte of English Poesie* (1589), 'the shorter the better' for such verses.

Ordinarily these poesies were romantic or religious. Of the more amorous examples uncovered in rings that survive from the period are 'Thee I chuse all others I refuse' and 'In thee my choys I do rejoys', fabulously concise expressions of romantic commitment.

One of the more serious and pious examples is a gold ring that survives in the collections of London's Victoria and Albert Museum, which bears the twin engraved inscriptions: 'OBSERVE WEDLOKE' ('Observe Wedlock') and 'MEMENTO MORI' ('Remember You Must Die'). Another, in Oxford's Ashmolean Museum, bears a reminder for the betrothed of their religious vow: 'as God decreed so wee agreed'.

In others are more personalized expressions of romantic emotion, with some light-hearted or even flippant. The genealogist Thomas Lyte (c.1568–1638) gave engraved rings to his two wives. That of his first wife, Frances Worth (d. 1615), whom he married on 2 February 1592, bore the inscription 'Lytes love is little worth', punning on her maiden name. Equally cheesy was the line on the ring he gave to his second wife, Constance: 'Constants be constant and the Lyte resplendant'.

WEDDINGS

The ring formed a central part of the solemnization of marriage as laid out in the 1549 *Book of Common Prayer*, which differed in important ways from Catholic practices, introducing a more reformed form of church service. The bestowing of a wedding ring on the bride's left hand was now fundamental to the vows exchanged between couples, the ring itself acting as 'a token or pledge'.

After the bride promised to take the bridegroom to be her 'wedded husband... to have and to holde from this day forwarde, for better, for woorse, for richer, for poorer, in sickenes, and in health, to love, cherishe, and to obey, till death us departe: accordyng to Goddes holy ordeinaunce', the rubric explained precisely what was to be done with the ring. The couple should lock hands, then the man marrying the woman took a ring, and other tokens such as gold or silver, and laid them on the book. The priest then took the ring and delivered it to the man, who put it on the fourth finger of the bride's left hand, saying: 'With thys ring I thee wed: Thys golde and silver I thee geve: with my body I thee wurship: and withal my worldly Goodes I thee endowe.' This marked a shift in practice from the Catholic Church, which until this point had traditionally stipulated that wedding bands be worn on the right hand. The fourth finger of the left hand was important, since it was thought by Tudor medics that it connected directly to the heart.

DEATH

While some rings signified romantic attachments between the living, others remembered the dead and departed. Memento mori rings given out at funerals were hugely popular during the sixteenth century. They commonly incorporated a skull motif, often with a black enamel background, and were engraved with death-related mottos or phrases which acted as rather stark reminders of the inevitability of death. A beautiful example of a gold memento mori ring, found in October 2006 in West Sussex, bears the simple but lingering and melancholy inscription 'know thyself'; while another, gold bezel memento mori ring found in March 2013 and dating from 1593 is inscribed 'LIVE TO DIE'.

These rings had often been designed and allocated by the deceased, which made both the gesture and objects themselves particularly potent. The judge Sir Anthony Browne (1509/10–67), for example, listed his friends – including Lord Rich – whom he wished to receive gold rings, which were to be engraved on the outside with the motto 'Wee dye' and on the inside, 'Forgett nott'.

Lord Rich (1496–1567)

A lawyer and civil servant who, almost uniquely, came out on the winning side during every twist and turn of Tudor political and religious upheaval. He was a merciless enforcer of the Reformation and a beneficiary of the Dissolution of the Monasteries under Henry VIII; became Lord Chancellor and was an unbending Protestant during the reign of Edward VI; went along with the plan to make Lady Jane Grey queen; supported the Catholic Mary I and turned his hand to burning Protestants; and then switched faiths again to support Elizabeth I.

A BEHEADED MOTHER

One of the most spectacular memorial rings to survive, and one heavily and unusually imbued with emotional significance, was a locket ring belonging to Elizabeth I – now held at Chequers, the country residence of the British prime minister. Comprising a mother-of-pearl band set with rubies and gold and an initial 'E' made up of diamonds, the ring also contains a secret compartment which, when opened, reveals two miniature portraits. One is of Elizabeth herself and the other is of her mother, Anne Boleyn, who was executed on her father Henry VIII's orders when Elizabeth was only an infant. The ring was said to have been removed from Elizabeth's finger after she died on 24 March 1603; she had worn it as a memorial to her mother.

JOIN IN!

We believe passionately that everyone – not just professional historians – can effectively exercise their historical imagination. If you have a great idea for a *Histories of the Unexpected* subject, fill in one of these forms, photograph it and send it to us

on Twitter **@UnexpectedPod**

or by email to **info@historiesoftheunexpected.com** and we might dedicate a podcast episode to you and your historical imagination!

The history of ______________________________ is all about...

____

The history of ______________________________ is all about...

____

The history of ______________________________ is all about...

____

The history of ______________________________ is all about...

____

The history of ______________________________ is all about...

____

SELECTED FURTHER READING

GENERAL

Bindoff, S. T., *Tudor England* (Harmondsworth: Penguin, 1950).

Brigden, Susan, *New Worlds, Lost Worlds: The Rule of the Tudors, 1485–1603* (London: Allen Lane, 2000).

Collinson, Patrick, *The Reformation: A History* (London: Weidenfeld & Nicolson, 2003).

———, ed., *The Sixteenth Century, 1485–1603* (Oxford: Oxford University Press, 2002).

———, *The Birthpangs of Protestant England: Religious and Cultural Change in the Sixteenth and Seventeenth Centuries* (London: Palgrave Macmillan, 1988).

———, and John Craig, eds, *The Reformation in English Towns, 1500–1640* (Basingstoke: Macmillan, 1998).

Eales, Jacqueline, *Women in Early Modern England, 1500–1700* (London: UCL Press, 1998).

Elton, G. R., *England under the Tudors* (London: Methuen, 1977).

Guy, John, ed., *The Tudor Monarchy* (London: Arnold, 1997).

———, *Tudor England* (Oxford: Oxford University Press, 1990).

Haigh, Christopher, *English Reformations: Religion, Politics, and Society under the Tudors* (Oxford: Clarendon Press, 1993).

———, ed., *The English Reformation Revised* (Cambridge: Cambridge University Press, 1987).

Heal, Felicity, *Reformation in Britain and Ireland* (Oxford: Oxford University Press, 2005).

———, and Clive Holmes, *The Gentry in England and Wales 1500–1700* (Basingstoke: Macmillan, 1994).

Houlbrooke, Ralph A., *The English Family, 1450–1700* (Harlow: Longman, 1984).

Ives, Eric J., *The Life and Death of Anne Boleyn* (Oxford: Wiley-Blackwell, 2005).

Loach, Jennifer, *Edward VI* (New Haven, CT: Yale University Press, 1999).

Loades, D. M., *Intrigue and Treason: The Tudor Court, 1547–1558* (Harlow: Pearson, 2004).

———, *The Mid-Tudor Crisis, 1545–1565* (London: Palgrave Macmillan, 1992).

Mackie, J. D., *The Earlier Tudors, 1485–1558* (Oxford: Clarendon Press, 1952).

Marshall, Peter, *Religious Identities in Henry VIII's England* (Aldershot: Ashgate, 2006).

Matusiak, John, *The Tudors in 100 Objects* (Stroud: The History Press, 2016).

Mendelson, Sara, and Patricia Crawford, *Women in Early Modern England, 1550–1720* (Oxford: Clarendon Press, 1998).

Palliser, D. M., *The Age of Elizabeth: England under the Later Tudors, 1547–1603* (London: Longman, 1983).

Rex, Richard, *The Tudors* (Stroud: Tempus, 2002).

Ridley, Jasper, *The Tudor Age* (London: Constable, 1988).

Ryrie, Alec, *Being Protestant in Reformation Britain* (Oxford: Oxford University Press, 2013).

———, *The Age of Reformation: The Tudor and Stewart Realms, 1485–1603* (Harlow: Pearson Longman, 2009).

Shagan, Ethan H., *Popular Politics and the English Reformation* (Cambridge: Cambridge University Press, 2003).

Tittler, Robert, and Norman L. Jones, eds, *A Companion to Tudor Britain* (Oxford: Blackwell Publishing, 2004).

Walsham, Alexandra, *Catholic Reformation in Protestant Britain* (Aldershot: Ashgate, 2014).

———, *The Reformation of the Landscape: Religion, Identity, and Memory in Early Modern Britain and Ireland* (Oxford: Oxford University Press, 2011).

———, *Church Papists: Catholicism, Conformity and Confessional Polemic in Early Modern England* (Woodbridge: Boydell Press, 1993).

Williams, Penry, *The Later Tudors, 1547–1603* (Oxford: Clarendon Press, 1995).

———, *The Tudor Regime* (Oxford: Clarendon Press, 1979; reprinted 1991).

1. THE CHAIR

Betteridge, Thomas, and Suzannah Lipscomb, eds, *Henry VIII and the Tudor Court: Art, Politics and Performance* (Farnham: Ashgate, 2013).

Kermode, Jenny, and Garthine Walker, eds, *Women, Crime and the Courts in Early Modern England* (Chapel Hill, NC: University of North Carolina Press, 1994).

Knecht, Robert, 'The Last Valois: A Tragic Story', *History Today*, 58/8 (July 2008).

Loades, D. M., *The Tudor Court* (Totawa, NJ: Barnes & Noble Books, 1987).

Starkey, David, ed., *Henry VIII: A European Court in England* (London: Collins & Brown, 1991).

———, 'Intimacy and Innovation: The Rise of the Privy Chamber, 1485–1547', in *The English Court: From the Wars of the Roses to the Civil War*, ed. D. R. Starkey (London: Longman, 1987), pp. 71–119.

Walker, Garthine, *Crime, Gender and Social Order in Early Modern England* (Cambridge: Cambridge University Press, 2003).

2. MONSTERS

Brammall, Kathryn M., 'Monstrous Metamorphosis: Nature, Morality, and the Rhetoric of Monstrosity in Tudor England', *The Sixteenth Century Journal*, 27/1 (Spring 1996), pp. 3–21.

Céard, Jean, 'The Crisis of the Science of Monsters', trans. Constance Spreen, in *Humanism in Crisis: The Decline of the French Renaissance*, ed. Philippe Desan (Ann Arbor: University of Michigan Press, 1991), pp. 181–205.

Crawford, Patricia, *Blood, Bodies and Families in Early Modern England* (Abingdon: Routledge, 2004).

Jordan, Constance, 'Woman's Rule in Sixteenth-Century British Political Thought', *Renaissance Quarterly*, 40/3 (1987), pp. 421–51.

Read, Sara, *Menstruation and the Female Body in Early Modern England* (Basingstoke: Palgrave Macmillan, 2013).

Redworth, Glyn, '"Matters Impertinent to Women": Male and Female Monarchy under Philip and Mary', *English Historical Review*, 112/447 (June 1997), pp. 597–613.

Richards, Judith M., 'Mary Tudor as "Sole Quene"?: Gendering Tudor Monarchy', *Historical Journal*, 40/4 (December 1997), pp. 895–924.

Shephard, Amanda, *Gender and Authority in Sixteenth-Century England: The Knox Debate* (Keele: Ryburn Publishing, 1994).

The Unabridged Acts and Monuments Online or TAMO (HRI Online Publications, Sheffield, 2011). Available from: http//www.johnfoxe.org [accessed: 05.02.18].

Walsham, Alexandra, *Providence in Early Modern England* (Oxford: Oxford University Press, 1999).

Wilson, Dudley, *Signs and Portents: Monstrous Births from the Middle Ages to the Enlightenment* (London: Routledge, 1993).

3. THE TOILET

Byrne, Muriel St. Clare, ed., *The Lisle Letters*, 6 vols (Chicago: University of Chicago Press, 1981).

Cockayne, Emily, *Hubbub: Filth, Noise, and Stench in England, 1600–1770* (New Haven, CT: Yale University Press, 2008).

Starkey, David, ed., *Henry VIII: A European Court in England* (London: Collins & Brown, 1991).

———, ed. *The English Court: From the Wars of the Roses to the Civil War* (London: Longman, 1987).

Thurley, Simon, *The Royal Palaces of Tudor England: Architecture and Court Life, 1460–1547* (London: Yale University Press, 1993).

4. ORANGES

Gerard, John, *The Autobiography of an Elizabethan*, trans. and ed. Philip Caraman (Longmans, Green and Co., 1951).

Kilroy, Gerard, *Edmund Campion: Memory and Transcription* (Aldershot: Ashgate, 2005).

Thirsk, Joan, *Food in Early Modern England: Phases, Fads, Fashions, 1500–1760* (London: Continuum, 2009).

Yates, Julian, 'Towards a Theory of Agentive Drift; Or, A Particular Fondness for Oranges circa 1597', *Parallax*, 8/1 (2002), pp. 47–58.

5. THE MIRROR

Archer, Harriet, and Andrew Hadfield, eds, *A Mirror for Magistrates in Context: Literature, History and Politics in Early Modern England* (Cambridge: Cambridge University Press, 2016).

Clucas, Stephen, ed., *John Dee: Interdisciplinary Studies in English Renaissance Thought* (Dordrecht: Springer, 2006).

Harkness, Deborah E., 'Shows in the Showstone: A Theater of Alchemy and Apocalypse in the Angel Conversations of John Dee (1527–1608/9)', *Renaissance Quarterly*, 49/4 (1996), pp. 707–37.

Paget, William, 'The Letters of William Lord Paget of Beaudesert, 1547–63', ed. Barrett L. Beer and Sybil M. Jack, *Camden Miscellany*, 25 (1974), pp. 1–141.

Slack, Paul, 'Mirrors of Health and the Treasures of Poor Men: The Uses of the Vernacular Medical Literature of Tudor England', in *Health, Medicine and Mortality in the Sixteenth Century*, ed. Charles Webster (Cambridge: Cambridge University Press, 1979), pp. 237–74.

Smith, D. B., 'The Mariner's Mirrour Part I', *Mariner's Mirror* (1913), pp. 50–2.

6. THE GIFT

Arnold, Janet, *Queen Elizabeth's Wardrobe Unlock'd* (Wakefield: Charlesworth Press, 1988).

Daybell, James, 'Lists of New Year's Gifts Given and Received by Henry VIII, 1539, and Elizabeth I, 1585 (Folger MSS Z.d.11 and Z.d.16)', in *The Pen's Excellencie: Manuscript Treasures at the Folger Shakespeare Library, A Festschrift on the Retirement of Laetitia Yeandle* (Washington, DC: Folger Shakespeare Library, 2002), pp. 32–5.

Fumerton, Patricia, 'Exchanging Gifts: The Elizabethan Currency of Children and Poetry', *English Literary History*, 53/2 (Summer 1986), pp. 241–78.

Glanville, Philippa, 'Plate and Gift-Giving at Court', in *Henry VIII: A European Court in England*, ed. David Starkey (London: Collins & Brown, 1991), pp. 131–5.

Hayward, Maria, 'Gift Giving at the Court of Henry VIII: The

1539 New Year's Gift Roll in Context', *The Antiquaries Journal*, 85 (September 2005), pp. 126–75.

Heal, Felicity, *The Power of Gifts: Gift Exchange in Early Modern England* (Oxford: Oxford University Press, 2014).

Lawson, Jane A., *The Elizabethan New Year's Gift Exchanges, 1559–1603* (Oxford: Oxford University Press, 2013).

McCracken, Grant, 'The Exchange of Children in Tudor England: An Anthropological Phenomenon in Historical Context', *Journal of Family History*, 8 (1983), pp. 303–13.

Murdoch, Tessa, *Treasures of the Royal Courts: Tudors, Stuarts and the Russian Tsars* (London: Victoria and Albert Museum, 2013).

7. WINDOWS

Beer, Barrett L., *Tudor England Observed: The World of John Stow* (Stroud: Sutton Publishing, 1998).

Brown, Sarah, 'The Survival, Preservation and Reinterpretation of the Medieval Stained Glass of St Mary's, Fairford, Gloucestershire', in *Art, Piety and Destruction in the Christian West 1500–1700*, ed. Virginia Raguin (Farnham: Ashgate, 2010).

———, *Stained Glass at York Minster* (London: Scala in association with the Dean and Chapter of York, 1999).

Gowing, Laura, *Domestic Dangers: Women, Words and Sex in Early Modern London* (Oxford: Clarendon Press, 1996; paperback 1998).

Marshall, Peter, ed., *The Impact of the English Reformation 1500–1640* (New York: Arnold Press, 1997).

Orlin, Lena Cowen, *Locating Privacy in Tudor London* (Oxford: Oxford University Press, 2007).

Whiting, Robert, *The Reformation of the English Parish Church* (Cambridge: Cambridge University Press, 2010).

8. HATS

Cooper, Tarnya, *Elizabeth I & Her People* (London: National Portrait Gallery, 2013).

Hayward, Maria, '"The Sign of Some Degree"?: The Financial, Social and Sartorial Significance of Male Headwear at the Courts of Henry VIII and Edward VI', *Costume: The Journal of the Costume Society*, 36 (2002), pp. 1–17.

Jansson, Maija, 'The Hat Is No Expression of Honor', *Proceedings of the American Philosophical Society*, 133/1 (1989), pp. 26–34.

Jones, Ann Rosalind and Peter Stallybrass, *Renaissance Clothing and the Materials of Memory* (Cambridge: Cambridge University Press, 2000).

Smith, Logan P., *The Life and Letters of Sir Henry Wotton* (Oxford: Clarendon Press, 1907)

9. BONES

Alsop, James D., 'Sea Surgeons, Health and England's Maritime Expansion: The West African Trade, 1553–1660', *Mariner's Mirror*, 76/3 (1990), pp. 215–21.

Butler, John, *Quest for Becket's Bones: The Mystery of the Relics of St. Thomas Becket of Canterbury* (London: Yale University Press, 1995).

Clowes, William, *A Prooued Practise for All Young Chirurgians* (London, 1588).

Duffy, Eamon, *The Stripping of the Altars: Traditional Religion in England, 1400–1580* (London: Yale University Press, 1992).

King, Christine, 'Shrines and Pilgrimages before the Reformation', *History Today*, 29/10 (October 1979), pp. 664–9.

Lawrence, Christopher, ed., *Medical Theory, Surgical Practice: Studies in the History of Surgery* (London: Routledge, 1992).

Pound, John, *Poverty and Vagrancy in Tudor England* (London: Routledge, 2013).
Tostado, Igor Pérez, '"The Godly Greedy Appetite": New Relic Circulation in the Early Modern World', *Cultural and History Digital Journal*, 6/1 (2017), pp. 1–12.
Walsham, Alexandra, 'Skeletons in the Cupboard: Relics after the English Reformation', *Past and Present*, 206/5 (2010), pp, 121–43.
Watt, James, 'Surgeons of the *Mary Rose*: The Practice of Surgery in Tudor England', *Mariner's Mirror*, 69/1 (1983), pp. 3–19.

10. LISTS

Brewer, J. S., Gairdner, J., Rodie, R.H, *et al.*, eds, (*Letters and Papers, Foreign and Domestic, of the Reign of Henry VIII*, 21 vols. and *Addenda*; 1862–1932).
Cromwell, Thomas, *Life and Letters of Thomas Cromwell*, ed. R.B. Merriman (2 vols, 1902).
Eco, Umberto, *The Infinity of Lists* (London: MacLehose Press, 2009).
Houlbrooke, Ralph, A., *English Family Life, 1576–1716: An Anthology of Diaries* (Oxford: Basil Blackwell, 1988).
Smyth, Adam, *Autobiography in Early Modern England* (Cambridge: Cambridge University Press, 2010).
Yeo, Richard, 'Notebooks as Memory Aids: Precepts and Practices in Early Modern England', *Memory Studies* 1/1 (2008), pp.115–36.

11. FIRE

Boynton, Lindsay, *The Elizabethan Militia, 1558–1638* (London: Routledge & K. Paul, 1967).

Cooper, Ian, 'Provincial News Networks in Late Elizabethan Devon', *Historical Research*, 87/237 (August 2014), pp. 404–22.

———, 'The Role of Devon's Militia during the Spanish Armada Crisis', *The Historian*, 116 (Winter 2012), pp. 16–20.

Cressy, David, 'Book Burning in Tudor and Stuart England', *Sixteenth Century Journal*, 36/2 (Summer 2005), pp. 359–74.

Duffy, Eamon, *Fires of Faith: Catholic England Under Mary Tudor* (New Haven, CT: Yale University Press, 2010).

Marshall, Peter, *Reformation England, 1480–1642* (London: Arnold, 2003).

———, 'Papist as Heretic: The Burning of John Forest, 1538', *Historical Journal*, 41/2 (1998), pp. 351–74.

Russell, Percy, 'Fire Beacons in Devon', *Transactions of the Devonshire Association*, 87 (1955), pp. 250–302.

12. EYES

Hearn, Karen, ed., *Dynasties: Painting in Tudor and Jacobean England, 1530–1630* (New York: Rizzoli, 1995).

Latour, Bruno, 'Visualization and Cognition: Thinking with Eyes and Hands', *Knowledge and Society: Studies in the Sociology of Culture Past and Present*, 6 (1986), pp. 1–40.

Strong, Roy, *The Cult of Elizabeth* (London: Thames & Hudson, 1977).

Strong, Roy, *Gloriana: The Portraits of Queen Elizabeth I* (London: Thames & Hudson, 1987)

Wood, Andy, '"A lyttull worde ys tresson": Loyalty, Denunciation and Popular Politics in Tudor England', *Journal of British Studies*, 48 (October 2009), pp. 837–47.

———, 'The Queen is "a goggyll-eyed hoore": Gender and Seditious Speech in Early Modern England', *The English Revolution, c. 1590–1720: Politics, Religion and Communities*, ed. N. Tyacke (Manchester: Manchester University Press, 2007), pp. 81–94.

13. THE FACE

Bertolet, Anna Riehl, 'Elizabeth I and the Heraldry of the Face', in *Elizabeth I and the 'Sovereign Arts': Essays in Literature, History, and Culture*, ed. Donald V. Stump, Linda Shenk and Carole Levin (Tempe, AZ: Arizona Center for Medieval and Renaissance Studies, 2011), pp. 189–99.

Cooper, Tarnya, ed., *Elizabeth I & Her People* (London: National Portrait Gallery, 2013).

———, *Citizen Portrait: Portrait Painting and the Urban Elite of Tudor and Jacobean England and Wales* (New Haven, CT: Yale University Press, 2012).

———, 'The Enchantment of the Familiar Face: Portraits as Domestic Objects in Elizabethan and Jacobean England', in *Everyday Objects: Medieval and Early Modern Material Culture and its Meanings*, ed. Tara Hamling and Catherine Richardson (Farnham: Ashgate, 2010), pp. 157–78.

Croft, Pauline, and Karen Hearn, '"Only matrimony maketh children to be certain...": Two Elizabethan Pregnancy Portraits', *British Art Journal*, 3/3 (Autumn 2002), pp. 19–24.

Hearn, Karen, 'A Fatal Fertility? Elizabethan and Jacobean Pregnancy Portraits', *Costume*, 34/1 (2000), pp. 39–43.

———, *Dynasties: Painting in Tudor and Jacobean England 1530–1630* (London: Tate Publishing, 1995).

Knapp, James A., ed., *Shakespeare and the Power of the Face* (Farnham: Ashgate, 2015).

Snook, Edith, '"The Beautifying Part of Physic": Women's Cosmetic Practices in Early Modern England', *Journal of Women's History*, 20/3 (Autumn 2008), pp. 10–33.

Strong, Roy C., *Tudor and Jacobean Portraits*, 2 vols (London: Her Majesty's Stationery Office, 1969).

14. BELLS

Bullinger, Heinrich, 'About the Ringing of Bells', in *Heinrich Bullinger, Schriften*, ed. Emidio Campi, Detlef Roth and Peter Stotz (Zurich: Theologischer Verlag Zurich, 2006), pp. 462–81.

Cattermole, Paul, *Church Bells and Bell-Ringing: A Norfolk Profile* (Woodbridge: Boydell Press, 1990).

Cooper, J. P. D., *Propaganda and the Tudor State: Political Culture in the Westcountry* (Oxford: Clarendon Press, 2003).

Craig, John, 'Psalms, Groans and Dogwhippers: The Soundscape of Worship in the English Parish Church, 1547–1642', in *Sacred Space in Early Modern Europe*, ed. Will Coster and Andrew Spicer (Cambridge: Cambridge University Press, 2005).

Cressy, David, *Bonfires and Bells: National Memory and the Protestant Calendar in Elizabethan and Stuart England* (London: Weidenfeld & Nicolson, 1989).

Hill, Robert Adam, 'The Reformation of the Bells in Early Modern England' (PhD thesis, Simon Fraser University, 2012).

Marsh, Christopher, 'Sacred Space in England, 1560–1640: The View from the Pew', *Journal of Ecclesiastical History*, 53/2 (April 2002), pp. 286–311.

North, Thomas, *English Bells and Bell Lore: A Book on Bells*, ed. William Beresford (Leek: T. Mark, 1888).

Postles, David, '"Ring Out Those Bells": Death and the Social Order in Early-Modern Leicestershire', *Transactions of the Leicestershire Archaeological and Historical Society*, 80 (2006), pp. 31–41.

Sheppard, Thomas, *The Lost Towns of the Yorkshire Coast* (Hull: Browns Savile Press, 1912).

Smith, Mark M., ed., *Hearing History: A Reader* (Athens, GA: University of Georgia Press, 2004).

Strong, Roy C., 'The Popular Celebration of the Accession Day of Queen Elizabeth I', *Journal of the Warburg and Courtauld Institutes*, 21 (1958), pp. 86–103.

Walters, Henry Beauchamp, *Church Bells of England* (Wakefield: EP Publishing, 1977).

15. SHRINKING

Akkerman, Nadine, *Invisible Agents: Women and Espionage in Seventeenth-Century Britain* (Oxford: Oxford University Press, 2018).

Blake, John, *The Sea Chart: The Illustrated History of Nautical Maps and Navigational Charts* (London: Conway, 2009).

Carey, Hilary M., 'Henry VII's Book of Astrology and the Tudor Renaissance', *Renaissance Quarterly*, 65/3 (2012), pp. 661–710.

Craig, L. A., 'Royalty, Virtue, and Adversity: The Cult of King Henry VI', *Albion: A Quarterly Journal Concerned with British Studies*, 35/2 (Summer 2003), pp. 187–209.

Howse, Derek, *Five Hundred Years of Nautical Science, 1400–1900: Proceedings of the Third International Reunion for the History of Nautical Science and Hydrography Held at the National Maritime Museum, Greenwich, 24–28 September 1979* (London: National Maritime Museum, 1981).

Johnston, Stephen, 'Making Mathematical Practice: Gentlemen, Practitioners and Artisans in Elizabethan England' (PhD thesis, Cambridge, 1994).

Lupton, Thomas, *A Thousand Notable Things, of Sundry Sortes Wherof Some Are Wonderfull, Some Straunge, Some Pleasant, Diuers Necessary, a Great Sort Profitable and Many Very Precious* (London, 1579).

McDermott, James, 'Baker, Matthew (1529/30–1613)', *Oxford Dictionary of National Biography* (Oxford: Oxford University Press, 2004).

Shields, David S., 'The Drake Jewel', *Uncommon Sense*, 118 (Spring 2004). Available from http://oieahc.wm.edu/uncommon/118/drake.cfm [accessed 05.02.2018].

Strong, Roy, *Artists of the Tudor Court: The Portrait Miniature Rediscovered, 1520–1620* (London: Victoria & Albert Museum, 1983).

Theilmann, John M., 'The Miracles of King Henry VI of England', *The Historian*, 42/3 (May 1980), pp. 456–71.

16. ACCIDENTS

Challis, Keith, 'Drowned in "a Whyrlepytte": The River Trent in the Nottinghamshire Coroners' Inquests of 1485–1558', *Transactions of the Thoroton Society of Nottinghamshire*, 108 (2005), pp. 115–23.

Cooter, R., and B. Luckin, eds, *Accidents in History: Injuries, Fatalities and Social Relations* (Amsterdam and Atlanta: Editions Rodopi, 1997).

Forbes, T. R., 'London Coroner's Inquests for 1590', *Journal of the History of Medicine and Allied Sciences*, 28/4 (1973), pp. 376–86.

Gibson, J., and C. Rogers, *Coroners' Records in England and Wales* (3rd edition) (Bury: The Family History Partnership, 2009).

Gunn, Steven, and Tomasz Gromelski, 'Everyday Life and Fatal Hazard in Sixteenth-Century England', ESRC-funded project at Oxford University. http://tudoraccidents.history.ox.ac.uk/ [accessed 08.02.18].

———, 'Sport and Recreation in Sixteenth-Century England: The Evidence of Accidental Deaths', *Sports and Physical Exercise in Early Modern Culture: New Perspectives on the History of Sports and Motion*, ed. Rebekka von Mallinckrodt and Angela Schattner (Farnham: Ashgate, 2016), pp. 49–64.

———, 'The Perils of Tudor Piety', *BBC History Magazine*, 16/7 (2015), pp. 51–5.
———, 'Deadly Beasts of Tudor England', *BBC History Magazine*, 14/13 (2013), pp. 43–7.
———, 'For Whom the Bell Tolls: Accidental Deaths in Tudor England', *Lancet*, 380 (2012), pp. 1222–3.
———, 'Toys and Games that Killed in Tudor England', *BBC History Magazine*, 13/13 (2012), pp. 37–40.
———, 'Drowning in Tudor England', *BBC History Magazine*, 12/13 (2011), pp. 46–9.
Tusser, Thomas, *Five Hundred Points of Good Husbandrie* (London, 1573).

17. FRUIT-EATING

Adams, Simon, ed., *Household Accounts and Disbursement Books of Robert Dudley, Earl of Leicester, 1558–1561, 1584–1586* (London: Cambridge University Press, 1995).
Dawson, Mark, *Plenti and Grase: Food and Drink in a Sixteenth-Century Household* (Totnes: Prospect Books, 2009).
Dyer, Christopher C., 'Gardens and Garden Produce in Later Medieval England', in *Food in Medieval England: Diet and Nutrition*, ed. Christopher M. Woolgar, Dale Serjeantson and Tony Waldron (Oxford: Oxford University Press, 2006), pp. 27–40, 28, 35–6.
Fitzpatrick, Joan, '"I Must Eat My Dinner": Shakespeare's Foods from Apples to Walrus', in *Renaissance Food from Rabelais to Shakespeare: Culinary Readings and Culinary Histories*, ed. Joan Fitzpatrick (Aldershot: Ashgate, 2010), pp. 129–36.
Lloyd, Paul S., 'Dietary Advice and Fruit-Eating in Late Tudor and Early Stuart England', *Journal of the History of Medicine and Allied Sciences*, 67/4 (2012), pp. 553–86.

Oppenheim, Michael, *A History of the Administration of the Royal Navy* (Aldershot: Temple Smith/Gower Publishing, 1988).
Thirsk, Joan, *Food in Early Modern England: Phases, Fads, Fashions, 1500–1760* (London: Continuum, 2009).
Winchester, Barbara, *Tudor Family Portrait* (London: Jonathan Cape, 1955).

18. LETTER-WRITING

Daybell, James, *The Material Letters in Early Modern England: Manuscript Letters and the Culture and Practices of Letter-Writing, 1512–1635* (Basingstoke: Palgrave Macmillan, 2012).
———, *Women Letter-Writers in Tudor England* (Oxford: Oxford University Press, 2006; paperback edition 2018).
———, ed., *Women and Politics in Early Modern England* (Aldershot: Ashgate, 2004).
———, ed., *Women's Letters and Letter-Writing in England 1400–1700* (Basingstoke: Palgrave, 2001).
Evans, Melanie, *The Language of Queen Elizabeth I: A Sociolinguistic Perspective on Royal Style and Identity* (Oxford: Wiley-Blackwell, 2013).
Gibson, Jonathan, 'Significant Space in Manuscript Letters', *Seventeenth Century*, 12/1 (1997), pp. 1–9.
Guillén, Claudio, 'Notes Toward the Study of the Renaissance Letter', in *Renaissance Genres: Essays on Theory, History, and Interpretation*, ed. Barbara Kiefer Lewalski (Cambridge, MA: Harvard University Press, 1986), pp. 70–101.
Stewart, Alan, *Shakespeare's Letters* (Oxford: Oxford University Press, 2008).
———, et al, *Letterwriting in Renaissance England* (Washington, DC: Folger Shakespeare Library, 2004).

Wall, Alison D., ed., *Two Elizabethan Women: Correspondence of Joan and Maria Thynne, 1575–1611* (Stoke-on-Trent: Wiltshire Record Society, 1982).
Williams, Graham, *Women's Epistolary Utterance: A Study of the Letters of Joan and Maria Thynne, 1575–1611* (Amsterdam: John Benjamins, 2013).
Wood, M. A. E., *Letters of Royal and Illustrious Ladies, from the Commencement of the Twelfth Century to the Close of the Reign of Queen Mary*, 3 vols (London: Henry Colburn, 1846).

19. CANNIBALISM

Brown, Jennifer, *Cannibalism in Literature and Film* (Basingstoke: Palgrave Macmillan, 2013).
Go, Kenji, 'Montaigne's "Cannibals" and *The Tempest* Revisited', *Studies in Philology*, 109/4 (2012), pp. 455–73.
Harmon, Alice, 'How Great Was Shakespeare's Debt to Montaigne?', *Publications of the Modern Language Association*, 57/4 (December 1942), pp. 988–1008.
Noble, L., *Medicinal Cannibalism in Early Modern English Literature and Culture* (Basingstoke: Palgrave Macmillan, 2011).
Sugg, Richard, 'Medicinal Cannibalism in Early Modern Literature and Culture', *Literature Compass*, 10/11 (November 2013), pp. 825–35.
———, *Mummies, Cannibals and Vampires: The History of Corpse Medicine from the Renaissance to the Victorians* (London: Routledge, 2011).
———, '"Good Physic but Bad Food": Early Modern Attitudes to Medicinal Cannibalism and Its Suppliers', *Social History of Medicine*, 19/2 (2006), pp. 225–40.

20. RINGS

Barton, Caroline, 'Mourning Rings: Portable and Poignant Souvenirs', British Museum Blog, 31 October 2013, https://web.archive.org/web/20150402162649/http://blog.britishmuseum.org/2013/10/31/mourning-rings-portable-and-poignant-souvenirs/ [accessed 08.02.18].

Cressy, David, *Birth, Marriage, and Death: Ritual, Religion, and the Life-Cycle in Tudor and Stuart England* (Oxford: Oxford University Press, 1997).

Duffy, Eamon, *The Stripping of the Altars: Traditional Religion in England 1400–1580* (London: Yale University Press, 1992).

Evans, Joan, *English Posies and Posy Rings* (London: Oxford University Press, 1931).

Tait, Hugh, ed., *7000 Years of Jewellery* (London: British Museum Press, 2006).

Taylor, Gerald, and Diana Scarisbrick, *Finger Rings from Ancient Egypt to the Present Day* (London: Lund Humphries for the Ashmolean Museum, Oxford, and the Worshipful Company of Goldsmiths, 1978).

ILLUSTRATION CREDITS

p. 1 *An Allegory of the Tudor Succession* by Lucas de Heere (*Wikimedia Commons*); p. 11 Woodcut of a cucking stool (*Wikimedia Commons*); p. 14 Witch-mark in a sixteenth-century house, Herefordshire, UK (*Alex Ramsay/Alamy Stock Photo*); p. 19 Woodcut of Argus sea monster in *Monstrum in Oceano Germanica*, 1537 (*North Wind Picture Archives/Alamy Stock Photo*); p. 27 A close stool, Hampton Court Palace (*Wikimedia Commons*); p. 33 Anthony Babington postscript in cipher (*The National Archives/Wikimedia Commons*); p. 39 Title-page of *The Mirror for Magistrates*, 1574 (*Public domain*); p. 47 New Year's gift roll of Elizabeth I, 1 January 1585 (*Folger Shakepeare Library*); p. 55 Reformation iconoclasm of the Calvinists in the Netherlands, etching by Franz Hogenberg, 1566 (*Rijksmuseum*); p. 58 Hardwick Hall, Derbyshire, UK (*Nicola Pulham/Shutterstock*); p. 63 Portrait of William Parr by Hans Holbein the Younger, c.1538–40 (*The Picture Art Collection/Alamy Stock Photo*); p. 69 Portrait miniature of George Clifford, 3rd Earl of Cumberland by Nicholas Hilliard, c.1590 (*Niday Picture Library/Alamy Stock Photo*); p. 71 Portrait of John Banister, c.1580 (*Wellcome Library, London*); p. 79 Shopping list of Michelangelo (*The History Collection/Alamy Stock Photo*); p. 87 John Foxe, *Acts and Monuments*: Martyrdom of Alexander Gouch and Alice Driver, 1558 (*The Picture Art Collection/Alamy Stock Photo*); p. 95 & p. 97 Elizabeth I's 'Rainbow Portrait', c.1600, Hatfield House (*Wikimedia Commons*); p. 101 Earl of Leicester's 'Eyebrows' in letter to Elizabeth I (*Folger Shakepeare*

Library); p. 103 Image from Henry's Psalter, British Museum (*World History Archive/Alamy Stock Photo*); p. 107 Pregnancy portrait of Katherine Carey, Lady Knollys (*Yale Center for British Art, Paul Mellon Collection*); p. 110 Elizabeth I's Armada Portrait, 1588 (*Chronicle of World History/Alamy Stock Photo*); p. 111 Hampton Court clock and bell tower (*Neil Lang/Shutterstock*); p. 119 The Drake Jewel, c.1586 (*World History Archive/Alamy Stock Photo*); p. 123 Shipwrights drawing, *Fragments of Ancient Shipwrightry* by Matthew Baker, 1586 (*Public domain*); p. 125 Engraving from Everard Digby's *De arte natandi*, 1587 (*Public domain*); p. 131 Portrait of Queen Elizabeth I by Steven van der Meulen, c.1563 (*GL Archive/Alamy Stock Photo*); p. 137 Portrait of Penelope Lady Rich by Nicholas Hilliard (*The Picture Art Collection/Alamy Stock Photo*); p. 143. *Os Filhos de Pindorama.* Cannibalism in Brazil in 1557 (*Wikimedia Commons*); p. 149 Portrait of Princess Elizabeth attributed to William Scrots, c.1546–7 (*Wikimedia Commons*)

While every effort has been made to contact copyright-holders of illustrations, the authors and publisher would be grateful for information about any illustrations where they have been unable to trace them, and would be glad to make amendments in further editions.

INDEX